D1569716

REGINALD F. LEWIS

Before TLC Beatrice

REGINALD F. LEWIS

Before TLC Beatrice

The Young Man Before The Billion-Dollar Empire

LIN HART

LHA Publishing Company
www.lhapublishing.com

ISBN-10: 0985347929
EAN-13: 9780985347925
Library of Congress Control Number: 2012947962
LHA Publishing Company, St. Louis, MO

DEDICATIONS

This book is dedicated to the memory of my parents Alice and Willie Hart and my daughter Gail Lynn Hart Stanfield. My parents dedicated their entire lives to making certain that my four brothers and I maintained a lifetime grip on all things right, fair, and decent.

Since her passing, at the age of 27, Gail's memory and her joyous spirit mark every day I live and everything I do.

It is also in memory of my high school coach and lifetime mentor, Julian Dyke. Coach Dyke chose to invest time and energy in me and in doing so, offered an able assist to my parents. It was his wish, that I become something more than just an athlete.

This book is also dedicated to the memory of Reginald F. Lewis, a friend who challenged me, frustrated me, yet inspired me. In so doing, he helped change the direction of my life for the better.

Reginald's life was a testimony that, though not easy, in our life-time it was possible to go as far as our dreams could take us. I hope that the same will be true in the future. It is in that spirit that I dedicate this book to my grandchildren, Rana Boyd, Brianna Stanfield, and Cameron James Hart.

PREFACE

Following my retirement from AT&T Network Systems in 1995, I traveled the country extensively as a businessman and professional speaker. During that time, I was frequently reminded, by audience responses and casual conversation that more needed to be said about Reginald F. Lewis's life. Someone needed to write a book that focused specifically on the years before Harvard, before Wall Street. As someone who had known Reginald as a neighborhood acquaintance, college roommate, and life-long friend, I felt this was a story I could tell. Our close association during this period had provided me with a front-row seat from which to witness the early stages of Reginald's remarkable and historic journey. Nonetheless, I resisted the urge to write such a book, thinking someone else might step forward to undertake the task.

At the urging of his widow, Loida Lewis, the late Dr. Purificacion Quisumbing, former chairperson of the Philippines Commission on Human Rights, and my wife, Frances Hart, I realized the time was right for me to write the story.

The pages of this book can only provide a brief glimpse into this remarkable man's life, but it will be a glimpse into a very important part of it. The timing of this book takes place when Lewis was first beginning to probe and test his theories about life and success. It was during this period that he was challenged to transform failure and disappointment into valuable lessons for life. He would also gain his first glimpse of the monumental task that lay ahead of him, if he was to achieve the ambitious goals he had set for himself. This book will reveal that long before Harvard or Wall Street, young Reginald F. Lewis had accepted the challenge. He began building his pathway to success early, and he never looked back.

The goal of this book is to serve as a beacon of hope and inspiration for those who wish to do as Reginald F. Lewis did, to begin the work of building their own pathway to success early and never look back. **Keep going, no matter what**!

ACKNOWLEDGEMENTS

The idea of writing this book was something I had thought about for years, but had never considered actually doing. Now that it is finished, I would like to acknowledge the special contributions of those who, in their own way, helped make this book possible.

At the top of the list of acknowledgments is my wife, Frances. Somehow, she always seems to know what transpires to be the best new direction for me to take. She was firm in her encouragement that I should write this book. Her time spent listening to me read passages from this book's manuscript and providing her unvarnished opinion was critical in helping me organize my thoughts in preparation for writing.

I would also like to acknowledge the role played by Loida Lewis, Reginald's wife, and by Reginald's mother, Mrs. Carolyn Fugett. After hearing me deliver a brief speech about Reginald, they both urged me to put my recollections about Reginald in book form. Knowing it was okay with the two of them was the nudge I needed. Knowing it was okay with them, provided the impetus for me to begin writing.

I owe a great deal to Dr. Purificacion Valera Quisumbing, former Director of the United Nations Centre for Human Rights, She was someone I had known for only a brief time. Yet, in a single evening, she posed the tough questions that helped me get beyond many of my own self-imposed barriers. I would like to acknowledge her for her wise counsel. She played a major role in bringing this book to life. Dr. Quisumbing passed away in December 2011.

Finally, I would like to acknowledge the special contributions of my nephew Roderick (Rick) Hart III, my son Lin Hart Jr., my brothers Roderick, Clarence, Gary, Willie Hart Jr., and my good friends Albert Banks and Herman Bell.

TABLE OF CONTENTS

PROLOGUE

In the spring of 2004, I was speaking to a group of Verizon Telecom employees at the Lord Baltimore Hotel in Baltimore. I had been traveling a lot, but I was really looking forward to having the opportunity to speak in my hometown. It gave me an emotional lift, as if I was attending my own homecoming party and being paid to attend. Baltimore always provided the perfect setting in which to acknowledge the accomplishments of one of the city's most successful natives, the late Reginald F. Lewis. It was always my practice to refer to Reginald whenever I was speaking to a large gathering. On this occasion, when I did so, there was an immediate show of interest by several people in the audience. They wanted me to say more, but I purposely kept my comments short. I was sensitive to the fact that Verizon had hired me to speak about teambuilding and the current challenges facing the telecommunications industry, not Reginald Lewis. Besides, this was something I had encountered many times before, and I knew there would be time for questions and answers following the formal part of the program. I always looked forward to having the opportunity to interact with the audience at that time.

At the close of my speech, I found myself being peppered by a volley of questions, covering a variety of issues. It came as no surprise to me that many of them were about Reginald. One of the last people to pose a question was a young African-American male, who had seemed particularly anxious to gain my attention. By the time he got an opportunity to ask his question, time constraints had forced us to end the session. As I was walking away, he caught up to me. He was short in stature and seemed to be standing on his tiptoes in an effort to establish eye contact. After I answered his first question, which had to do with the telecom industry, he quickly threw out a second. This one I had not anticipated. With a big, broad smile on his face he said, "If Reginald Lewis grew up in East Baltimore and the west side, he must have been one tough dude." I was caught off guard by his comment, and for a moment I had to give pause. Given the topic of my talk, "Team Building," I was not expecting a question having to do with Reginald's toughness.

I smiled, asking him "Do you mean tough as in street tough." "Yes," he replied. I laughed and said, "I would have no way of knowing if he was or wasn't. In all the years that I had known him, I never saw him in a street fight. Now, if you had asked me if he was a fierce competitor, my answer would have been an unequivocal yes. Reginald Lewis was always trying to win, but his most effective weapon was never going to be his fist. It was going to be his mind. Inside his head, he would have been 100% certain that whatever the stakes, his chances of winning were always going to be better than yours." The young man seemed pleased with my answer. He thanked me and walked away.

My brother Rod, a retired Verizon employee, had accompanied me during the speech. He had volunteered to serve as my camera operator for the morning. While collecting our equipment, I kept thinking how odd it was that I had not gotten the one question I had always gotten before. It had come up more than any other question, when audiences became aware of my association with Reginald F. Lewis. This was especially true of the younger members of the audience. Maybe it was because this was Baltimore, Reginald's hometown, but for whatever reason the question had not come up that morning.

As I was checking out of the hotel, I noticed a small group approaching me. I recognized a couple of people as having been part of the Verizon audience. The missing question may have been late getting there, but it was about to arrive. The first question they asked was, "What was Reginald Lewis like before he became so rich." The answer to that question is what this book seeks to address.

While not claiming to provide the complete and definitive answer, I sincerely believe that a significant part of the answer to that question lies within the pages of this book. If nothing else, I believe this book will go a long way toward bringing more understanding to those seeking to know more about this phase of Reginald F. Lewis's life.

CHAPTER 1:

WHY THIS BOOK?

"What was he like?" Jack Kennedy said the reason people read biographies is to answer that basic question.

One evening, I was sitting at my desk staring out at the pictures mounted on the wall behind my computer monitor. The wall seemed like a deep, vast sea of emptiness. I was having one of my rare moments of writer's block. Just at that moment, the phone rang. It was my nephew, Roddy, on the end of the line. He was calling to see if I had a minute to speak with his 12-year-old son, Rick. I saw this as the much-needed rescue I was longing for. I always enjoy talking with Rick. He is an impressive kid for his age. Rick is blessed with a light-bulb personality, which, when combined with his inquisitive nature, can cause a room to light up the minute he walks in. His insatiable appetite for information means you never know just where you're going to end up with Rick. He took the phone, saying he was working on his black history project. He and his classmates had drawn their subject's names randomly and he had picked Reginald F. Lewis. He said, "When I saw I had drawn Reginald Lewis's name, I went 'Oh Wow! My uncle Linwood knew this guy. He'll be able to help me write this report.'" He then asked if I had a few minutes to answer some questions. I said, "Sure, fire away."

I now found myself engaged in a fascinating discussion with this exuberant and inquisitive 12-year-old. Rick was like a sponge for information, and he was hanging on to my every word. His questions were thought provoking. The two of us were enjoying our own walk back in time. I thought it was great, having this opportunity to share my experiences with Rick. As we were winding down our conversation, I promised to send him a copy of a photo I had kept around for years. It was a photo of Reginald and me standing together in front of an aluminum Christmas tree. For a moment, I felt like I needed to explain the site of that glimmering, aluminum Christmas tree in the background, but I figured Rick would likely corner me on that one on my next visit back home to Baltimore. My wife, Frances, had taken the picture in our small apartment in 1966, when Reginald was home on Christmas break from Harvard.

Rick was ecstatic. Not only did he have the benefit of my firsthand accounts, but he would also have this photo as part of his presentation. I told him I was sending the photograph because I wanted him to get an A on his project. He promised me he would deliver that A. As we were hanging up, he thanked me repeatedly. Twelve-year-old Rick was off to continue working on his project, but thanks to his probing questions I had been inspired. My writer's block had vanished as if it had been a mere puff of smoke. I was excited at the prospect of this book finding its way into the hands of some young reader like Rick. Maybe it would inspire them to seek more knowledge and a greater understanding of events going on around them. Who knows? They might even choose to begin their own journey along the path that ends up turning their dreams into reality, just as a young Reginald F. Lewis had done many years before. There was pure magic in the thought. As I was hanging up the phone that evening, I paused for a second, thinking, "I now know why I have to write this book."

Who Was Reginald F. Lewis?

Reginald F. Lewis was born and reared in Baltimore, Maryland. He was a product of both the Baltimore city Catholic and public school systems. Upon graduation from Dunbar High School in 1961, he attended Virginia State University in Petersburg, Virginia. He graduated from Virginia State in 1965. He then entered Harvard University, graduating in 1968. Reginald began his career as a lawyer with the New York firm of Paul, Weiss, Rifkin, Wharton & Garrison. He would later open his own firm in 1970, Lewis & Clarkson, specializing in venture capital projects.

Reginald achieved an extraordinary record of success as a lawyer, businessman, and entrepreneur. His knack for finding business opportunities resulted in two prominently heralded acquisitions, the first being his $22.5 million deal to buy McCall's Patterns in 1984. He would later sell McCall's in 1987 for $65 million, making a 90 to 1 return on his investment. His next deal was his stunningly successful leveraged buyout of Beatrice Foods' international business operations in 1987 for $985 million. When Reginald made the acquisition, Beatrice was a company with annual sales in excess of $2 billion, making him the successful bidder in the largest international leveraged buyout ever executed in the United States. Beatrice had 64 companies in 31 countries. When you make that kind of deal, people start referring to you by your initials. Thus, RFL had arrived.

RFL arrived on Wall Street with a pretty big bang. He would later rename the company TLC Beatrice, with offices and plants located throughout Europe and the Far East. Following the purchase, Reginald surprised many who had underestimated his intentions. Prior to his deal, the typical leveraged buyout was destined for the auction block. The acquiring party would proceed to break up the company and sell off the various parts. The prevailing belief stemmed from the idea that, once broken up, the pieces of the company would be worth more than the whole. Many before Reginald's successful buyout of Beatrice had worked this idea to perfection. However, in his typical, "Don't try to figure me out" style, he chose to go against conventional thinking after acquiring the assets of Beatrice. Following the initial sell-off of a portion of the assets, he set out to run the company for profit. Not everyone was happy with this strategy, but as its CEO and chairman, he navigated TLC into a period of improved financial and operational success until his sudden death in 1993. He had continued to build upon his personal wealth. At the time of his death, his personal wealth was estimated to have been in excess of $400 million. This was serious wealth not just for an African-American: it was serious wealth for anyone.

Considering the magnitude of Reginald's financial success, it would be reasonable to ask, "Why this book?" Why write a book about young Reginald F. Lewis? Wouldn't it be a more interesting and noteworthy book if it focused on the behind-the-scene details of how this stealthy African-American businessman muscled his way into the backrooms of Wall Street's dealmakers? Wouldn't it be great copy to reveal how he pulled off one of the biggest international leveraged buyouts in history? The answers to both questions are quite simple.

It is not a book I could have written, even if had wanted to do so. I was never behind the closed doors when those dealings were going on. Moreover, the definitive book covering the events associated with that period of Reginald's life has already been written. Prior to his death, Reginald began a process that resulted in the writing of his autobiography.

Throughout the pages of this book, there will be times when I will describe Reginald Lewis as being unreasonable, argumentative, and downright arrogant. It's true, if you knew him as I did, you knew he could be all of those things. However, there will be other instances in this book in which I will present him as a charismatic and ambitious guy, who could become a study in brilliance when brilliance was required. When Reginald was on his game, he could focus like a laser on matters of importance and brilliantly assess his opportunities. As you will see from reading this book, he was also someone who was capable of demonstrating real empathy and compassion when it came to friends and family.

I have always believed that the lessons he learned and the obstacles he overcame during the period covered in this book had much to do with shaping the man Reginald F. Lewis eventually became. Yet, it is a period about which very little has been written.

In reading this book, you will find that nearly all of my accounts are first-hand. The focus of this book will be on a specific 10-year period of Reginald's life, between 1956 up until his admission to Harvard Law School. While we remained friends throughout the course of his life, this was a period during which we were particularly close. It is the period during which we first met and it extends through high school and beyond our college years together at Virginia State College, (now Virginia State University). There are a few brief references to incidents that took place beyond those years, but this book is mainly about Reginald F. Lewis, the multimillionaire business tycoon, before he became rich.

Historic Accomplishment

Reginald Lewis's accomplishments were significant, but as an African-American, they were historic. It was always his tendency to play down this point, choosing not to dwell on race.

Former Maryland State Delegate Clarence "Tiger" Davis, a high school football teammate of Reginald's, recalls a discussion he had with Reg following the announcement of his Beatrice deal. He had run across his old pal following a meeting in Maryland and offered his congratulations on the deal. During their discussion, he extended credit to Reginald for having helped to open the door for black businessmen on Wall Street. According to Davis, Reginald was quick to respond. He said, "I would prefer that you not refer to me as a 'black' businessman." He said, "Such terms were typically used to pigeonhole people in ways that tended to diminish their accomplishments. I've always thought of myself as a businessman, capable of competing on any level and with anybody." Davis says he was caught off guard by the strength of Lewis's protest but acknowledges that there was a certain real-world truth to Lewis's claim.   Having heard Reginald tell many stories about "Tiger" Davis in the past, I knew that Davis was someone Lewis thought highly of, but this was a point on which Reginald held strong convictions.

I had always understood why he felt this way. By the time Reginald completed his deal for Beatrice, in 1987, I had racked up over 20 years working for the largest corporation in the country, AT&T. I had spent a good deal of that time witnessing racial stereotyping being used as a means of denigrating the contributions of African-Americans in the workplace. Reginald Lewis was a proud man, and he wanted to make certain his achievement was allowed to stand on its own merit.

Still, for millions of people like Tiger Davis and myself, there was no getting around the historical significance the Beatrice deal and Reg's role in it held for African-Americans. It was an event that had a major impact upon the collective psyche of African-Americans. Reginald Lewis was an African-American. He was one of us, and when the news of his buyout of Beatrice's international assets hit the front pages of the *Wall Street Journal* in 1987, it was an absolute blockbuster. Here was this black guy who many had never heard of, and he had just achieved something that no one, black or white, had ever achieved.

He had successfully pulled off the largest international leveraged buyout in U.S. history. There was no way this was not going to become an immediate source of pride for African-Americans throughout the country. I do not believe this fact was ever lost on Reginald. In a quote he made following his ascent to the front pages of nearly every major publication in America, he seemed to acknowledge as much. This quote appeared in the *New York Times,* January 20, 1993, following the announcement of his death,

"I'm very proud of the accomplishments of African-Americans," Mr. Lewis said in an interview shortly after the acquisition of Beatrice. "And I'm delighted that people feel this accomplishment adds to that list."

Ever aware of his public image, he went on to say *"But to dwell on race -- to see that as something that becomes part of my persona -- is a mistake, and I do everything I can to discourage it."*

At the time of his death in 1993, he was well on his way to becoming America's first African-American billionaire.

People Need to Know about This Guy

In 1995, I began my second career. After retiring from AT&T, I became a professional speaker and business coach. I continued my practice of making certain I always shared Reginald's story with audiences. I did this because I could always foresee the likelihood of his success. When I first began doing it, Reginald was a relative unknown. People in the audiences back then would often comment, "I've never heard of this guy. Why do you think he's so important?"

Following his acquisition of McCall's Patterns, this began to change. I had my first inkling that things were about to change in a big way in 1986, while a participant in Yale's Executive Management Program. One evening, I found myself caught up in a dinner discussion amongst a group of visiting business executives. They had traveled up to Yale from New York that evening. We were all scheduled to participate in a session on business finance the next day. The highlight of the evening for me was to be seated next to the late Bart Giamatti. Mr. Giamatti was making a special visit to Yale after having served as the school's president from 1978 to 1986. He had just been appointed president of the National Baseball League. We had struck up a conversation on business and baseball during cocktails, and he suggested that we sit together at dinner. This was a stroke of luck I had not counted on. As you might imagine, he was the ideal dinner guest. We both shared a keen interest in sports and business.

At some point during the evening, one of the dinner guests entered Reginald F. Lewis's name into the broader dinner table discussion. I decided to avoid revealing that Reg and I were friends, not wanting to influence the comments coming from participants around the table. I was interested in hearing what these men really thought about Reginald. Most of the questions and comments buzzing around the table were typical of the ones I had heard before. That is until one of the dinner guests, a grey-headed distinguished-looking gentleman with the appearance of a senior partner, spoke up. He chimed in, "You guys haven't seen anything yet. This guy Lewis is on his way to becoming a multi-millionaire." I figured Reg was already worth more than a couple of million, but hearing the term "multi" associated with the word "millionaire" had a significant impact on me. It was a call to sit up and take notice. Reginald F. Lewis had come a long way since his days on Mosher Street. As they say in the neighborhood, I realized that this brother was about to blow up big time.

During a subsequent phone call, I mentioned this to Reginald. He replied in a somewhat joking manner, "It's nice to have people mentioning my name, but they are just wasting a lot of their time if they are talking about me." Knowing him as I did, I never for a minute believed that he meant what he was saying. By that time, his name was starting to gain some real traction in business circles. Reginald was savvy enough to know that being mentioned in a large audience of prominent business people was a good thing. As long as he could keep his personal life beyond the prying eyes of a curious public, everything would be fine. Having people showing this kind of interest in him would fit nicely with his self-image.

After his death, I began noticing a new kind of interest developing with respect to Reginald's life. People in the audiences I was speaking to still remained curious about his business achievements, but there was increasingly an interest in his development as a young man. I began hearing questions like, "What were the qualities that made him so successful?" "Where did he grow up?" "Why am I just hearing about him?" "How did he get injured in college?" Most of these questions were coming from young people in the audience, who were beginning to be inspired by his story.

An example of how this played out can be seen in this story, which took place in the spring of 1997. A couple of weeks had passed since my appearance on a St. Louis television show. I received a call from a young man who identified himself as Charles Sallee. At the time, Charles was working for Ralston-Purina. Ralston- Purina has since been merged with Nestlé and is now known as Nestlé Purina PetCare. Charles said his boss had watched the TV show and had sent him to hear me at an event where I was scheduled to speak. Charles having heard me, his boss now wanted to know if I would be available to speak to his organization. Charles arranged a meeting between the two of us so that we could work out the details of the engagement. I was both surprised and pleased to find that his youthful boss, James White, had been an admirer of Reginald Lewis.

During our meeting, James proudly announced that he had read Lewis's autobiography. He said Lewis's story had served as an inspiration for him in his efforts to carve out his own career as a successful businessman. Upon hearing this, I told him that I had known Reginald Lewis and that before his death we had been friends. After a long conversation, I agreed to speak to James's team. This marked the beginning of a long friendship and coaching relationship between young James White and me.

James White, a young businessman, had been inspired by Reginald's story. James has since moved on from The Nestlé Company and has proceeded to carve out an impressive track record as a corporate leader. He has held senior executive positions with Gillette, Procter & Gamble, and Safeway. He is currently serving as the chairman and CEO of Jamba Inc., a global healthy food and beverage company headquartered in Emeryville, California.

There have been others, like Larry Penn III. Larry is a young man I have known since he was an adolescent. His parents, Rachel and Lawrence Penn Jr., have been friends of my family for years. As a high school student, young Larry would often seek me out just to discuss Reginald Lewis. Much like Reginald, Larry was highly motivated and possessed a passion to succeed. He would ultimately enter West Point, where he continued to study Reginald's career in great detail. Larry graduated from West Point in 1992. After serving his tour of duty in the military, he returned to civilian life. Following his passion and inspired by Lewis, he headed straight for Wall Street as he had always planned. Today, Larry serves as the Managing Director of The Camelot Group, a New York–based private-equity firm.

Both James and Larry, two young African-American businessmen, would be among the first to tell you their lives have been positively impacted by Reginald's story. They are both among today's emerging leaders. In the years since Reginald's death, I have heard countless stories, received many questions, and listened to numerous personal testimonies that validate the positive impact his story has had upon the lives of young men and women.

CHAPTER 2:

MY FIRST RFL SIGHTING

"Dress for where you're going, not for where you've been."
Lin Hart

By 1952, Baltimore city leaders could see that they would need to do more to accommodate the city's expanding African-American population. City officials reluctantly agreed to target certain areas as being available for black residency. West Baltimore was a primary target area.

In October of 1952, my family was among the first black families to move into this predominantly white area. Our new address was 1218 North Dukeland Street. It was in West Baltimore, in the area city planners referred to as the Dukeland-Rosemont area. In those days, the area was a pleasant well-developed blue-collar community made up predominantly of white families with a smattering of black families. It had tree-lined streets and close proximity to schools, churches, and small businesses. Many of our friends were white kids whose families had chosen to stay because they could not afford to move. Our friendships with white kids did not last very long. Over the next five years, spurred by the influx of more blacks moving in and the resultant white flight, a dramatic change in the racial composition of the neighborhood took place. In a span of 10 years, the neighborhood was nearly all black.

In the years that followed, the neighborhood would undergo many changes. In the early stages, many of them were for the better. The new homeowners took great pride in their homes and especially in their lawns, which were immaculate and uniformly trimmed. I have many fond memories of growing up in the neighborhood. As the years wore on, other changes were not so kind to the neighborhood and its remaining homeowners. Still, it would remain the place of residency for my parents for nearly 53 years.

Growing up in racially polarized West Baltimore in the early 1950s meant understanding and respecting some well-defined boundary lines. Even as more black families moved into our neighborhood, my pre-teen friends and I continued to remain close to home. One of the main reasons for this was the vacant lot at the end of the street where I lived. At that time, the now defunct Formstone Company owned it. For years, the company had specialized in making a unique stone facing used on many of the old row homes in Baltimore. As a kid, this seldom used property served as a place of recreation, where my friends and I spent countless hours playing baseball and football.

In 1956, Reginald's path and mine would cross for the first time. Circumstances would dictate that we would not meet until then. Neither of us was aware of the other's existence. We had been living only a few blocks away from each other since 1952, when his family relocated from East Baltimore. Reginald's Mosher Street address was just at the outer edges of where most of my neighborhood friends lived and played. I spent very little time in his part of the neighborhood, and even if this had not been the case, it was unlikely I would have met Reginald any sooner.

After his family relocated to Mosher Street in West Baltimore, Reginald continued to spend most of his time in his former East Baltimore neighborhood. It was where his friends lived and when Reginald was not working, he was in East Baltimore.

Dukeland Street, where I lived, was frequently the chosen path of pedestrian foot traffic traveling North and South. Those walking along this route would have to pass right past my front porch.. This provided me with the perfect perch from which to peer at many of the new faces moving into the neighborhood. The rate of white flight taking place in the neighborhood made people-watching an interesting pasttime for a curious teen-ager.

It wasn't long before I began noticing this new kid making an occasional trip past my house. He always walked at a measured pace, with his eyes fixed straight ahead. He seemed friendly, but he didn't say very much. Occasionally, he would offer the obligatory "What's up?" or "How's it going?" but it was rarely more than a few words. There was one thing about him that quickly drew my attention. He didn't dress like most kids in my neighborhood. It wasn't that kids in my block didn't dress neatly; it just seemed that this kid was usually dressed up. Shirt, tie, dress shoes, and neatly pressed slacks. He had what, in the 1950s, we called the "Collegiate Look," and it seemed to be permanently painted on. This was my first sighting of young Reginald F. Lewis.

I later learned from his mom that those trips past my house were part of his routine visits to see his aunt and his grandparents. They had just moved to their new West Baltimore residence, several blocks away on Ashburton Street. By taking the shortcut past my house, Reginald could shave 10–15 minutes off his walk.

At first glance, I thought, "This is not a friendly guy," but after thinking about it I took a somewhat different view of him. Reginald was street savvy. He knew the smart play, when in a new neighborhood, was to say very little, avoid attracting a lot of attention, and keep moving.

As time passed, our paths would cross more frequently, largely due to our mutual interest in sports. We would eventually compete against each other in high school sports. It was then that we became better acquainted. We were not yet close friends, but we were cordial because we recognized each other from the neighborhood.

Reginald's mother, Mrs. Carolyn Fugett, said, "Reginald walked a lot in those days." Given his tendency to work hard and save his money, the determined teenager would ultimately end up buying his own car. One of the things I would soon learn about Reginald was his firm belief that his car was his private domain and not to be confused with the local taxi service. There was never a lot of joy-riding in his prized new possession. When it came time to decide who would get to ride in his car, he had a simple, yet effective, rule. He was fond of saying, "If you didn't walk with me when I was walking, you can't ride with me now that I'm riding."

His former Dunbar teammate Leon Stewart put it this way: "Reg wasn't anti-social. He just chose not to hang out with everybody." Reginald was always predictable when it came to relationships. He always wanted to be the one who would set the terms of the relationship and the terms of the deal.

Playing with the Big Boys

In the summer, kids on my block and the adjacent streets played baseball every day. After a few years of knocking around each other on the Formstone Company lot, we decided we were respectable enough to play in the city recreational league. At the same time, we realized we were a few players short of having a truly competitive team. The word went out to find a few good players from playgrounds nearby. Extending our reach beyond the lot was going to be a significant challenge. For most of us, we had never played on a conventional baseball diamond. Though the lot had served us well, it really wasn't a baseball field. It was an old abandoned space sandwiched between the railroad tracks and the brick homes that lined Ellicott Drive. The train tracks ran atop the hill, just beyond third base. The hill formed what a baseball enthusiast might refer to as our version of the "Green Monster" in Boston's Fenway Park. It wasn't green and there was no wall; instead, there was a big hill with train tracks. Any ball hit up on that hill and onto the railroad tracks was usually lost and considered an automatic home run. Thinking through our plan to enter the more competitive Baltimore Recreational League forced us to own up to having a number of needs. We discovered that we were not only in need of players, we were also desperately in need of baseballs, a new field, a sponsor, a coach, uniforms, and transportation.

We lucked out when it came to finding a sponsor. One of the growing numbers of new residents in the neighborhood was Mrs. Dorothea Langley. Mrs. Langley lived on Ellicott

24

Drive. She was an older woman, in her late fifties, and she held considerable clout within the local Democratic Party. She agreed to sponsor us, but there was one catch. The team had to be named The Ellamont Giants, after her old neighborhood and her local political affiliation. This made no sense to any of us, but that was the deal. Take it or leave it. Given the sorry state of our finances and our organizational dysfunction, we took it. It turned out to have been a good deal for everyone. Mrs. Langley worked tirelessly on our behalf. She procured equipment, coaches, and permits to allow us to practice on the public fields at Bloomingdale Park. She even got us a fair deal from the Department of Recreation when it came to scheduling our home and away games. Now we needed to get a few better players. This is where Reginald Lewis came in.

I didn't know if he could play or not, but there was one thing you could say about Reginald Lewis: He was not a particularly big guy, but he looked like an athlete. His short, stocky build, confident strut, and his serious demeanor suggested that he might be a good ball player. One day I saw him walking past my house, carrying a baseball glove and spikes tossed over his shoulder. I decided to put the recruitment pinch on him. I asked him if he would like to play on our team. He said he was already playing for a team and politely turned down my offer. Afterwards, I discovered he was playing on the same team as my cousin, Harold. Harold was the catcher for Reginald's team and he was nearly three years older than I was. I knew a few other guys on that team and they were a much older group. I thought, Reginald didn't look that much older than I did. How was it that he was playing with these guys?

This bit of confusion stuck in my memory, causing me to assume Reginald was much older than he really was. It also fit with something else I was beginning to notice about Reg. Whether it was in the neighborhood or in high school athletics, it seemed like he was consistently playing up a notch or two. He was always playing with the older and better guys. He played baseball, basketball, and football at Dunbar, and much of his playing time was spent on the varsity team. There was also a level of maturity in his conversation. It far exceeded that of the average 15- and 16-year-old guys I was hanging out with at the time. It was a short jump for me to conclude that he was a much older guy. I carried this mistaken impression with me until we became roommates. It was then that I discovered we were closer in age than I had thought. We were both born in December, with his birthday being December 7, 1942, and mine being December 28, 1943. I would often kid him, claiming his mustache made him look 10 years older than me. It never seemed to bother him.

Reginald's history of having played with older and bigger guys was a subject of immense pride for him. While in college, he would hold court well into the night describing how he had played on Dunbar High School teams with some of the most talented seniors when he was in the ninth grade. He contended that having played with the big boys, or "Playing Up," was one of his proudest accomplishments. It would later become a critical component of his thinking, insisting that playing with the big boys, or "Playing Up," always made you a better player.

CHAPTER 3:

THE MAKE-UP OF THE YOUNG MAN

"Granular understanding of complex problems is what separates the geniuses from everyone else. They know that details do matter."
Lin Hart

It is often written that Reginald F. Lewis burst upon the scene of American business like he'd come out of nowhere. Reginald was an incredibly private person, which fed into this narrative and perhaps lent some credibility to this idea. Reginald's life was distinguished by many qualities, two of which stand out prominently for those who knew him well: his need for privacy and his tendency to be somewhat difficult to work with at times. These were always consistent parts of his make-up, but in that respect he was far from unusual.

A closer look at Steve Jobs's long history of success with Apple computers reveals that he always clung to privacy as a centerpiece of his strategy. It was said by those who knew Jobs well that, though brilliant, he was a difficult person to work with, too. When he was dismissed from Apple, he went on his own and started another computer company called NEXT. The products created at NEXT were far from sensational, but during his time at NEXT, Jobs refined a business strategy that he applied often and effectively over the rest of his career. In an episode of Bloomberg's show *Game Changers*, Robert X. Cringely, a technology journalist and former Apple employee, said, "While at NEXT, Jobs discovered that he got more attention by being secretive than he did by being open, and he actually did not have much to show. Being secretive made it appear that he had more than he actually had."

Starting as a young man, this was a philosophy Reginald F. Lewis always adhered to. He understood that revealing too much information about your plans could eventually cost you in the long run. Keeping his stuff private and operating under the radar had its benefits. Very few people I grew up with or who came to know Reginald during his time on Virginia State's campus actually knew much about him, his family, or his economic status. They were always left to decide for themselves, and Reginald was very good at creating the image he wanted you to see.

Depending upon who you talk to, you can get a variety of opinions about what Reginald Lewis was like. I suppose that is as it should be, because when all is said and done, we all have our good days and our bad days.

The Right Attitude for Reaching the Right Altitude

Reginald possessed the right attitude for where he was headed. From the beginning, I had very little doubt that Reginald F. Lewis was going to be a success. In many ways, his success was due as much to what he was not as it was to what he was. He was not a gifted student, but that motivated him to work tirelessly to overcome this particular shortcoming. He was not a physically overpowering person, but he drove himself to become an extremely tough-minded person. He did not have a lot of money, but he went to great lengths to carry himself in a manner that made it look as if he did. While in college, he was never one of the most popular people on campus, but his friends were notable and popular.

Like most people, Reginald had his share of faults. One of his most glaring faults was his tendency to judge others too quickly. At times he could be curt and even dismissive of someone he held in low regard. On this point, Reginald would tell you he never needed, nor wanted, many friends. He was not a good loser, but publically he handled losing gracefully. He absolutely hated losing. The idea of losing was a complete anathema to him. There were times when he just exploded after something had failed to go his way. To his credit, most of those times were in private.

It would have been easy to find a few holes in his style and his delivery, but his attitude was the right attitude for where he was headed.

A Master of Charm

Among his many exceptional talents was one special gift that, over the years that I knew him, never failed him. Reginald was the absolute master of charm. This was especially true if you were someone he liked or held in high regard. When it came to engaging others in conversation, he was never at a loss for words. Never mind the topic, Reginald had an opinion on everything, and more often than not, he was masterful in presenting it. He would use this skill often and effectively.

My mom and dad had met Reginald on only a handful of occasions, usually on brief stopovers at my house before we headed off someplace in his car. On each occasion, he would always find some way to impress my mom with his manners and politeness. She would say, "That Reginald Lewis is really a nice boy." It wasn't that I disagreed with her assessment, but there were times when Reginald had his charm machine turned on so high I thought he was prepping for the priest-hood. It was as if he had developed a case of "terminal nice-ness."

His talents, as a charmer, were never more evident than in those moments when an attractive woman would show up. He could be in the middle of a heated debate, firing on all cylinders, but let a fine young lady show up and his transformation was nothing short of miraculous, even though it was as predictable as day following night. In an instant, Reg would roll out his patented "Red Carpet Charm," behaving every bit like the legendary lover/seduc-er Don Juan. Watching him operate in such instances was something to behold.

While some may have been less impressed with this aspect of Reginald's behavior, I always liked the fact that he could flip the switch like this. I believed it was one of the key reasons we got along well. We were two very opinionated guys, often willing to engage in verbal duels at the drop of a pin. Still, we took great pains to make certain we kept our friendship intact. Recognizing his ability to transition easily from one emotional state to another was a critical part of learning how to co-exist with Reg. He could be angry about something but quickly table the argument. I recognized the importance of being able to do this, but he was better at turning down the heat than I was. There were never any grudges or long periods of unsettled disputes. We patched up disagreements and quickly moved on. I can't say this was the way he dealt with everyone, but it was the way we kept it real, between the two of us.

You Gotta Track and Measure Stuff

When we first became roommates, I couldn't help noticing how extremely disciplined Reginald was. He kept track of everything. It was an ongoing habit. He would collect the cardboard inserts that came with our laundered shirts and tear them into sections. He would then use them to draw up his monthly calendar or scribble out his schedule for the week. He would use notes and paper pads to track appointments, study times, test grades, etc. This was his way of keeping track of how he was doing, and he was remarkable in his ability to keep all this stuff up to date.

Reginald was a born competitor, so keeping score was important to him. Sometimes he would be competing against you and you would not know it. He had a habit of always asking what my grades were, while being slow to reveal much about his own grades. Though my grades were good, I was never one to discuss them openly with others. With Reginald, such discussions were unavoidable. He would always put on the full court press around grades time, asking, "What did you get? What did you get?" I always held my ground, insisting, "If you show me yours, I will show you mine." He would eventually ease off. Reg was a born competitor, and this was his way of trying to see how he stacked up against others.

Reginald struggled mightily with his grades during his time at Virginia State. Even he would admit that his grades were not up to his liking in his early years. However, it was my observation that it was not from a lack of study. He put in the study time, and I could never understand how he was not able to get a better return from the time he invested. Even so, I was never among those who wondered, "How could someone of such modest academic accomplishments achieve such extraordinary success in business and finance?" Whether in sports, the classroom, or in a frat room discussion, Reginald Lewis enjoyed the minutiae of details. Pearl Bobo recalls what it was like being in a class with Reginald. She says, "He had a tendency to dominate a classroom discussion if not closely monitored by professors." She did not know Reginald at the time but could not help noticing his habit of pressing his side of the discussion for unusually long periods of time. Pearl recalls turning to a classmate and both of them wondering aloud, "Who is this guy and why is he always taking up so much of our class time?" That was Reginald Lewis.

Whether it was recalling what happened during the course of a game, analyzing someone's behavior, or arguing his point of view, he had this rather annoying habit of dragging up minute scraps of detail to support his point. The more time we spent together, the more I noticed the variety of ways in which he relied upon detail. There were times when it was clear that he was pounding people with detail.

I would often observe, with great interest, someone engaging him in a debate or argument for the first time. They had no idea what they were getting into. As the debate grew more intense, I knew that this person was about to be overwhelmed by a withering assault of facts, historical accounts, and a blizzard of repetitious detail. In the rare instance where his adversary would begin to hammer away at those details, Reg was not above blowing a little smoke (making up stuff) to jack up the heat on the person. It was worth the price of admission just to see it all unfolding. Every disagreement or debate was a cause for him to take a deep dive into an ocean of detail and to drag the other participants with him. Initially, I saw this habit as a personal weakness, but in retrospect it turned out to have been one of his greatest strengths.

I would be the first to admit that the sheer magnitude of Reginald's wealth and success far exceeded my expectations, but those who knew him well were aware that he possessed an outsized ego and ambition, which in the end played a big role in his extraordinary success.

Sam Chisholm, former CEO of the Chisholm-Mingo Group and a classmate at Virginia State, recalls Lewis having a taste for the finer things in life, long before he became a man of wealth. Reginald's appetite for fine style and taste had been whetted by stories he had heard from his grandfather, Sam Cooper. Mr. Cooper had served as a waiter in some of Baltimore's most prestigious hotels and country clubs.

Chisholm recalls how Reginald's favorite pair of shoes had been his thick-soled English Oxfords. In the 60s and 70s, the shoe was very popular among high school and college prep types in Baltimore. The shoes featured a wing-tipped lotus design on the toe, which led many to refer to them mistakenly as "loaders." Chisholm says, "I remember him going on and on about his shoes one day. He kept raving about how his thick-soled English shoes were top of the line. He said they were the best money could buy. I thought it was unusual that a guy would go on like this about a pair of shoes." Chisholm was one of Lewis's best friends at Virginia State. Like many of his friends, there were times when you were somewhat amused by Reginald's actions, but you always knew there was a level of seriousness coming from him that you could not ignore.

The more time I spent with Reginald, the more aware I became of the many people who had been influences in his life. First, there were his grandparents, aunts and uncles, and coaches, but there was one person who stood out more than any other. She was, in my opinion, the catalyst that fueled Reginald's intense drive and ambition. It was his mother, Mrs. Carolyn Fugett.

I recall first meeting her in 1961, and I was surprised by her youthful looks. I made the mistake of telling Reginald that I thought his mom was attractive. The scowling look of disapproval he gave me in return quickly communicated his dissatisfaction with my comment. I was caught off guard by his reaction, but I made a mental note to not go down that road again. When it came to his family, and especially his mom, Reginald was extremely protective.

From the first moment I met his mother, it was easy to tell that she was a no-nonsense woman, and her effect upon Reginald was undeniable. She nurtured him and instilled in him the right attributes, and it showed throughout his life. Among the most notable were:

1. Develop a strong, positive self-image. Wherever you choose to go in your life, always act and feel like that is where you belong.

2. Have the courage to demand more from yourself than anyone else ever will.
3. Possess the curiosity to extract meaning from all of life's experiences.
4. Make it your business to earn your own way in the world and never rely upon someone else to do it for you.

At the core, this was young Reginald F. Lewis.

Reginald had learned early in his life that success would come from having the discipline to cultivate an awareness of what was going on around him and an appreciation for detail. His questioning nature was important. It is a quality we always see among highly successful people. Curiosity is what allows them to extract meaning from what others might regard as unrelated events. By diving deep into subjects, Reginald could come to understand the details. This was his way of connecting the dots. It provided the answers to the always-elusive questions: why, how, and when. Reginald knew that by applying the proper level of scrutiny, the answers to these three questions would reveal themselves in ways that would lead to better outcomes. The consistent application of these principles would come together to form the basis for his mental model for success.

"an endless piling up of minutiae, an almost ferocious tracking down of ions, electrons and molecules, an unshakable determination to tell it all. One is amazed by the mole-like diligence of the man."

H.L. Menken, describing the writing of Theodore Drieser

Young RFL's Mental Model

Reginald's mental model served as the prism through which he saw himself, his life, and the world around him. It gave him the perspective to see how he fit in. His mental models were his inside pictures of the outside world. They shaped his views on work, people, politics, success, and making money.

Experts tell us that we all carry around within us our personal mental model of the world we live in. These models serve as our moral compass with respect to what we see, what we think, and what we believe to be correct. For some of us, our mental model can become our biggest source of problems. The problem stems from the fact that the world and the environment around us is in a constant state of change. With all the modern technologies of today, the change is taking place at an exponential rate. It forces each of us to take a periodic re-evaluation of what we believe, just to make certain our mental models are keeping pace. Those who fail to do this run the risk of becoming blind to new opportunities and new possibilities. Reginald understood that managing one's mental model was a full-time job. It can make the difference between knowing what beliefs to hold onto and which ones to relinquish.

As early as the 1960s, Reginald Lewis had adopted a mental model that said the world was going to undergo massive change and he needed to prepare for a different kind of future and a different world. He understood that many of the barriers of that day were destined to fall. In his vision for the future, he would not be satisfied watching this change dynamic play out from the sidelines. He was determined to play a lead role, thus becoming an agent of change and for that to happen he would have to view the world as a place where opportunities abounded, just for the taking. The world had to be seen as a place where anyone could succeed beyond their wildest dreams, if only they could become dreamers. Not just wild-eyed dreamers, though: They would have to become focused, enthusiastic, and well-intentioned dreamers. They would have to be able to visualize themselves achieving their dreams and actually becoming successful. This was never going to a difficult task for Reginald F. Lewis.

Reginald was determined not to take a pedestrian view of the world. He was going to be a full participant. The way he went about it brings to my mind a quote I recall hearing from George Lucas, the brilliant movie director. When questioned about his unique ability to come up with creative and lucrative ideas, Lucas replied, "I never try to think outside the box. I don't even want the box." That was young Reginald.

CHAPTER 4:

THE SUMMER OF 60 SETS UP THE SUMMER OF 61

"History never looks like history when you are living through it."
John Gardener

The summer of 1960 was a pivotal time in bringing the two of us closer together. By 1960, Reginald and I had become neighborhood acquaintances, but we had not yet become close friends. There were two events, both occurring in the summer of 1960, that would help facilitate our friendship the next year.

The first of those events involved my brother Rod's decision to join the Air Force in June 1960. The second event was far more troubling, and it would leave an imprint on my memory that is as fresh today as it was the day it happened.

When I first became aware that Rod had signed up to join the Air Force, I had a feeling of mixed emotions. He had just graduated from Baltimore City High School, and I was pleased that he was doing something he had always wanted to do. Still, I was somewhat reticent, considering the impact it was going to have on our relationship. Rod was 17 months older than I was, and until this point I had never known a time when we were not together. He was my constant companion. Whether it was playing sports, going to parties, roaming the neighborhood, or getting into neighborhood scraps, we did it together.

Rod was bigger than I was and much more restrained in temperament. He was solidly built and he could handle himself well in the occasional scrap with the neighborhood toughs. I was thinly built and more the wiry type. This made Rod's presence even more important to me. When it came to needing an emergency backup, he was like the head of my customer services department. Whenever one of the older, bigger neighborhood toughs started to push me around, they would always have to weigh the prospect of coming face to face with the head of my customer services department. At that point, all complaints and disputes would eventually come to a screeching halt. The so-called tough guys would come down with a sudden case of dementia and end up forgetting about pushing the matter further. They would usually end up settling for a rain check, rather than having to deal with the head of customer services. Of course, there was more to our relationship than Rod being my defender. He was also my best and closest friend.

Now that he was going away for a four-year military hitch, I had to forge a brand new routine. Where I had been content with hanging out with Rod and his older friends, I would now have to reach out to make a few new friends my own age. It was something I had never contemplated before. With Rod leaving, I knew my summers were never going to be the same.

The second critical event of the summer of 1960 occurred a few weeks before Rod was scheduled to report for duty at Lackland Air Force Base in Texas. I was attending a neighborhood party when a ruckus broke out between my friends and a group of guys from a different part of town. As is often the case, the shoving match began over a seemingly innocent act. It had flared up when one guy stepped on another guy's shoes. Before you knew it, there was a challenge issued and a call for a showdown following the party. Showdowns always ended up with a fight.

Rod had joined the party later that evening. I really did not expect anything to happen, but it was reassuring to know that I would be well covered if a fight broke out. As the party was letting out, a series of troubling events began to unfold. At first, it was nothing more than a stare-down contest from competing sides of the street. Then it escalated into guys yelling obscenities and threats at each other. At some point during all of this, a neighborhood kid named Steward emerged from his house. Steward was 14 or 15 years old at the time. His timing could not have been worse. As he emerged from his house to observe what was going on, he had the misfortune of being on the wrong side of the street. He further put himself in harm's way when he decided to leave his house to go look for his older brother. This meant he had to walk through this group of guys. As he approached them, there was a heated exchange of words between Steward and several of the boys in the group. Before we knew it, a pushing and shoving match broke out. Steward was thrown to the ground and quickly overwhelmed by the entire group. Without giving much thought, my brother and I, along with several friends, bolted across the street to help Steward. What happened after that was just a blur, with guys throwing punches and wresting each other to the ground. The fight lasted only a matter of seconds, but it seemed much longer. I have no recollection of hearing a siren, but someone yelled "The Cops," at which point we all took off running.

This had been a crazy, hot summer's night. Exhausted and sweating profusely, Rod and I both made it to the front steps of our house. As we sat there, out of breath, gazing into the night sky, we both started laughing. What we were laughing about may be difficult for some to fathom, but it was the thought that the police probably had failed to catch up to anyone. It may sound strange to some, but as a black teenager growing up in a racially changing neighborhood in 1961, running from the cops was something of a sport. Rod and I were never in any trouble with the police before or after this event, but we grew up knowing that whenever the police showed up, you ran. You ran, even when you knew you had not done anything wrong. Not to do so could end up with you being caught and charged with doing something you hadn't done. We both found a bit of humor in thinking how close we had come to being caught by the cops this time, but like all the other times before, we had made it home okay.

The morning of the next day, a Sunday, I recall my mom bursting into our bedroom yelling, screaming, and shaking like I had never seen her before. Growing up in our house, it had become standard procedure for my mom to roust Rod and me from bed on Sunday mornings. Sunday mornings meant Sunday school and church. This time, though, it was different. She was more animated and in a high state of stress. What she then said, upon entering our room, still reverberates in my head today. She screamed, "What do you boys know about that boy who got killed last night?" What we thought had been a scuffle between a few hot heads had actually been a knife fight, resulting in the stabbing death of Steward. He had died earlier that morning. I remember being so scared, but at the same time feeling lucky to be alive. It's a moment that sticks with me to this day, and it's unlikely that I will ever forget it. The police later determined that both Steward and his assailant had knives. Steward's assailant was later released on a plea of self-defense.

In the months that followed, the situation in the neighborhood became increasingly dangerous, as there were threats of retaliation on both sides. It all happened so fast and was so tragic. How could Steward be gone forever, and how could something as senseless as a spat over some guy stepping on another guy's shoes have led to this? Thinking about all that had happened in the summer of 1960 brought me to the conclusion that I had to make some changes in my routine. With Rod leaving for a 4-year hitch in the Air Force and the tragic events of Steward's death behind me, I knew I would have to change things. I decided I would now have to find a way to reach out to discover some new friends. Socially, I made a commitment to be more proactive in reaching out beyond the boundaries of my old neighborhood, which at that time represented the limits of my comfort zone. I realized that my summers of innocence were now behind me, and the summer of 1960 had set up the summer of 1961.

Al and Me plus Reggie Makes Three

As the summer of 1961 approached, I began to wonder how I would spend my time. I had just come through my first school year without my brother, Rod. Now, I would have to go it alone for the first time in my life. I started by focusing my efforts on finding a summer job. Once that was done, I still had a large space to fill. My mind would occasionally wander back to events of the past year. There were still bitter feelings among certain neighborhood rivals, emanating from the death of Steward. In the city, bad feelings seemed to fester more in the hot days of summer. Rumor had it that a few guys on both sides of the issue were still looking for revenge. It seemed like a good time to set some new routines. What I really needed to do was reach out in an effort to establish some new friendships. As fate would have it, Reginald Lewis was about to emerge as a central figure in my life. In the past we had been casual acquaintances, but now we were about to become good friends.

The summer was just beginning when I received a phone call at my home. The guy on the other end of the line was Reginald Lewis. He said he had heard I was going to Virginia State on a football scholarship. After he congratulated me, he proudly announced that he had also received a football scholarship to attend Virginia State. He said, "I've been following you, and I know you made the All State Team as a receiver. You know, the two of us could really raise some hell down at Virginia State this season." Actually, I had been a runner who had caught a lot of passes coming out of the backfield, but that didn't matter. Having played with a couple of the best receivers in the city, Leon Stewart and Bill Tinkler, Reginald knew the value of having capable pass receivers on his team.

I thought to myself, he's right about the likelihood of us being able to raise some hell down at Virginia State. I had played against Reginald while he was at Dunbar High School, and I knew this guy could really throw the football. In high school he had established himself as one of the best quarterbacks in the city. I asked him if he was aware that the quarterback from my high school team, Al Banks, would be going to Virginia State too. He said, "Yes. I had heard that." My initial thought was, "Wow! Both of these guys are great quarterbacks, and they both love to throw the football. As a receiver, I'm going to be like a pig in slop." I was excited for all three of us.

We hadn't been on the phone long before Reggie put a proposal on the table. He said, "What do you say we get together and lay out a schedule for working out together this summer. I can work on my passing, and you can work on your pass catching and route running." I said, "That sounds good to me. I'll contact Al to see if he can join us." Reg said, "Great. Let's do it." Just like that, a big part of my new summer routine was now in place. The summer of 1961 was off to a great start. A passing acquaintance had now moved from familiar acquaintance and was about to become a good friend.

After a couple of workouts, it soon became evident that this setup was not going to work out exactly as we had planned it. While we all lived in West Baltimore, we all had summer jobs in different parts of the city. I figured logistics would inevitably come into play and I was right. That summer, I worked at nearby Lutheran Hospital, which was walking distance from my house. My route to work carried me right by Reggie's house every day. It also meant I was within walking distance of Bloomingdale Park, where our workouts would be taking place. It was a different story for Al. He had a long commute to get to his job as a short order cook at a fast food joint in East Baltimore and he was required to work evenings. Al only made a couple of our summer practice sessions. Reginald worked as a waiter in the Suburban Club, a prestigious gathering place for some of the wealthiest families in the city. The logistics were not going to be a problem for him, because he had the big difference maker when it came to getting around town. He had a car, "The Hillman," a used British model automobile. Having his own wheels allowed Reg to get around town a lot easier than either Al or me.

On those infrequent occasions when Al did join us, the footballs would be flying all over the place, and there was always a side discussion going on. Most often, those discussions were just a lot of guy talk about the local sports scene. One topic that always seemed to get the most airtime was the running debate over who were the best legendary Baltimore city high school athletes. These were guys who, down through the years, had demonstrated superior talent and total dominance within their respective sports. Their final ranking among this pantheon of high school greats was heavily dependent upon a particular skill or strength that distanced them from all the other competitors of their day.

It didn't take long for these to become highly charged and partisan debates. Reg would always stack the list with a lot of guys from Dunbar. Dunbar High School had been around for years, and it had carved out a long history of having produced some of the finest high school athletes in Baltimore. As graduates of a 4-year-old high school, Al and I were at a considerable disadvantage when it came to coming up with a similar list of alumni heroes. That still didn't stop us from engaging in spirited debate.

The "hardest runner" category got most of the attention during these discussions. I attributed this to the fact that Al and Reg were quarterbacks, and quarterbacks hated tackling anybody. Though blessed with powerful barrel legs and a stocky build, tackling was not Reginald's strong suit. He was quick to remind people that he was a quarterback and that quarterbacks didn't get paid to tackle runners. At 175 lbs., I was always a willing tackler, but I had to admit that tackling some of the guys who made our list were among my worst nightmares.

The name most frequently mentioned in the hardest runner category was Robert Cheeks, a running back from Baltimore's Douglas High School. Cheeks always won the top vote in this category. It was never even close. We chose him because he was big, fast, strong and had a fierce running style. Robert Cheeks was a 250 lb. "Mountain of a man" playing a boy's game. For us, the thought of having to tackle Cheeks one on one, in the open field, was a scenario we never wanted to face. Reginald would jokingly claim that there were guys all over Baltimore city who'd had their IQs lowered from trying to tackle Bobby Cheeks. Fortunately for us, Cheeks graduated in 1957, a couple of years before we arrived on the varsity high school football scene. We were all glad we never had to tackle that guy. We would soon come to find out that all of this talk about the hardest runners would take on a greater meaning for each of us in the days ahead.

These workout sessions provided my first glimpse of the Reginald Lewis I would come to know later. I could see that winning a debate or argument of any kind was important to him. If you happened to be the person on the other side of the debate, you would soon feel as if someone had tied one hand behind your back and pushed you into a fight with an octopus. He could be relentless and unyielding.

Note to self: Winning an argument with Reginald F. Lewis is never going to be easy.

The Royal Theatre

Reginald Lewis was not a guy who hung out a lot. Still, there were times when we would linger long after our workouts, discussing a wide range of topics. Unless he was heading in a different direction, he would always offer me a ride home. I was really beginning to enjoy his company, and I could see he enjoyed spending time, working on his passing game. I suspect there were a few other reasons the pairing was working out. Aside from living close by, I didn't smoke, drink, or do drugs, and I had been a good student and successful high school athlete. From my perspective, Reginald was an easy guy to hang out with, too. He was bright, talked nonstop, and had an opinion on everything. Of course, there were times when he would begin to take off on one of his big success theories and I would simply zone out. I hate to admit it, but at that stage of my life, going to college was more about playing football than dreaming exotic dreams of how I was going to conquer the world. On this point, we were quite different.

We managed to get past these temporary communication speed bumps because, to my surprise, Reginald possessed a great sense of humor. It took a while to show up, but when it did, it was always accompanied by his big trademark laugh.

On those few occasions when he would stop by my house, we would spend time hanging out on my front porch with a few of my friends. My oldest brother Willie Jr. became the butt of my kidding for years for having once, chastised Reginald for referring to him by his nickname, June. The incident occurred one afternoon, when Reginald and I were joined by a couple of my friends sitting on my front steps. June, who was 11 years my senior, was a great guy, but at times could be a bit surly. As he was approaching the steps that day, I casually called out, "Hey June." Reginald had never met my brother, but he took this as his cue to do likewise. When Reg chimed in, "What's up June," my brother turned to him and said, "What do you mean June. You don't know me that well." This resulted in Reginald having a somewhat embarrassed look on his face. While I'm certain Reginald had long forgotten about the incident, I never let my brother live it down. I would frequently kid him about having told the richest black guy on the planet, "You don't know me that well." He could do nothing but laugh.

By the summer of 1961 , Reginald had enough prominence in Baltimore high school sports that most of the guys in my block knew who he was. Reg never had any problem fitting in. There were times when he would call me and say, "Hey! I've got to go over to East Baltimore. You want go with me?" Usually, my answer was, "Okay. Let's Go." As far as I could tell, those trips were nothing more than a way for Reginald to kill some time or to check up on his buddies on the East Side of town. The lead-up to these road trips always left me with the impression that we going to where the girls were. We usually ended up meeting up with a few of his football buddies or stopping by his father's small restaurant. If they served any other purpose, I missed it. Still, I could never be sure. As time passed, I discovered that Reginald was not someone who openly discussed everything he was doing. His mother, Carolyn Fugett, says, "Reginald always liked to keep his personal business close to his vest." In this, he succeeded magnificently.

I recall casually tossing out the suggestion that we should attend a rhythm and blues stage show at Baltimore's venerable Royal Theatre. I didn't know it at the time, but Reggie was mainly a jazz enthusiast. Since he had never exhibited any interest in R&B or rock and roll, I thought he would quickly dismiss the idea. To my complete surprise he said, "Hey! That sounds like a good idea. Let's do it."

For years, the Royal Theatre had been the place to go for black entertainment in Baltimore city. It was well renowned for having served as the venue of choice for such fabled entertainers as Red Fox, Duke Ellington, Count Basie, Cab Calloway and Baltimore's own Billie Holiday. The Royal Theatre was one of the main stops on what used to be known to African-Americans as the "Chitlin Circuit." The circuit included other well-known black theaters like the Howard in Washington, D.C., and Harlem's famous Apollo Theater.

As the 60s rolled around, the typical African-American teenager's taste was just beginning to make the turn toward R&B. Baltimore's Royal Theatre had become a favorite venue for rhythm and blues entertainers like Otis Redding, Jackie Wilson, James Brown, Ray Charles, and the Coasters. It was located on Pennsylvania Avenue, which at that time had a reputation for being a tough place. Heroin use and gambling were growing in Baltimore, and Pennsylvania Avenue was ground zero for drug trafficking. The area had long been marked as the exclusive territory of the city's drug kingpin, Little Melvin Williams, and other lesser players. Unless you knew your way around the area, you were putting yourself at considerable risk attending a night show at the Royal Theatre. You had to be careful not to stare at anyone too long, bump into anyone, or step on anyone's shoes. Doing any of those things was just about a guarantee you would get your ass kicked.

Hearing Reginald's enthusiastic "Let's do it" left me wondering if Reg Lewis, "The Preppy Guy," really understood the risks associated with attending a night show at the Royal. For me, the logic of attending was clear. I was a big fan of R&B, so going to the show under any circumstances was going to get big thumbs up from me. Headlining the show was Smokey Robinson and some guy named Chuck Jackson. Neither of us knew anything about Chuck Jackson at the time, but a Smokey Robinson show was just too good to pass up.

On the night of the show, we had a long wait standing in line. Most of the folks in line were just like us; they just wanted to see a good show. However, a few guys in that line looked as if they could start pounding the crap out of people without much cause or provocation. We came perilously close to bumping heads with one of them. Fortunately for us, our wait was uneventful. Once inside the theater, I quickly noticed the emergence of a new Reginald Lewis.

He became some guy I was not used to seeing. Maybe it was the music, but this was the first time I had seen him completely let his guard down. When the smooth sounds of R&B started to flow through the rafters of that sacred hall, the formal Reggie was gone. This new guy standing beside me was officially open for business. Without the benefit of drugs, booze, or any other kind of mood-altering substance, it was smooth sailing for the rest of the evening for the both of us. Reginald and I were totally committed to having fun that night.

For the entire show, the music and the dazzling stage lights created the feel of a big party. Reginald joked and laughed freely about his lack of rhythm and his inability to dance. We both spent way too much time in a bizarre conversation about what constituted "cool." I was of the opinion that when it came to partying, "cool" was a combination of being a good dancer and good looking. In my opinion, this was the winning combination when it came to getting the girls. Reg held a different opinion. He suggested that when it came to getting the eye of the ladies, being a good dancer had nothing to do with it. It was all about the way you looked and the way you looked at a woman. It was all about striking the right pose at the right moment. This he referred to as his "Killer Pose." He contended that under the right circumstances, his brand of cool could get any woman in the house at any time. He claimed that it was all about timing and the way you looked at a woman. With guys like Jackie Wilson, Smokey Robinson, Marvin Gaye, and Sam Cook driving the R&B train in those days, it was possible to make a strong case either way. This was entertaining, but the real answer was going to show up in the second half of the show

Then Came Chuck Jackson

Of all the names featured on the marquee outside the Royal Theatre that night, one made no impression on either of us. His name was Chuck Jackson, and at that time we didn't know who he was. However, he was just a few minutes away from making a serious impression on Reginald. When Jackson took the stage that evening, Reginald became more convinced than ever as to the correctness of his definition of "cool." Chuck was standing there, right in front of us, and in Reggie's mind he was the very personification of his definition. Up to this point, Reginald had been an unabashed jazz fan. At least for that moment, R&B was making an impression upon Reginald Lewis, and it was considerable. It would be evident throughout the early years of our friendship.

When Chuck strolled onto the stage, he didn't make many dance moves. A step here, a step there, but most of the time, he was just singing. His appearance was immaculate. He was wearing a perfectly fitted suit, perfectly matched shirt, sparkling cufflinks, and polished shoes with a sheen so bright they practically blinded you with the reflection of the stage lights. To top it all off, Chuck was performing his newly released hit song, "I Don't Want To Cry." At one point in the song, Chuck turned and gave an adoring look to the ladies in the front row. The response was immediate and resounding.

You had to be there to appreciate it. In Reg's mind, this was the "Killer Look," he had spoken about. At that point, he leaned over to me and said, "See that. That's what I'm talking about. It's the look." For him, his definition of cool had been confirmed and validated. He simply could not stop talking about how cool Chuck Jackson looked that night.

If you are old enough to have been around when Chuck Jackson was at the top of his game, it was easy to see what Reginald was talking about. Jackson had a great stage presence and a smooth delivery in everything he did on stage. Aside from having a great voice and a cool look, he could deliver a song in a way that made every guy in the audience want to be him and every woman in the audience want to be with him. His killer look had an edge to it that seemed to say, "I've got my stuff together, and I know I can have any woman in this place." There it was. That was the Reginald Lewis image of cool, right there up on that stage, personified by Chuck Jackson. Over time, I would come to understand that Reg's admiration for Chuck Jackson's style and performance revealed much about how he viewed himself.

I never knew what kind of person Chuck Jackson was in real life. However, for that moment, on stage with all those girls screaming and shouting, he was the guy Reginald wanted to be. He was not a loud, boisterous, attention-grabbing figure up there on that stage. Yet, when he made his entrance, you couldn't avoid asking, "Who in the hell is that guy?"

When Reg and I became roommates, I always had my portable transistor radio close by. Whenever that song was on the air, Reg would jump to his feet and slide into his groove.

This was something that closely resembled dancing. His first move would be a slow shuffling of his feet. It was not always pretty, nor was it in time with the music, but so what? Reg was good at a lot of things, but dancing was not one of them. His second move was a rolling shake of his shoulders, accompanied by a side-to-side movement. This would continue for the length of the song, while never occupying more than one square foot of floor space. It was efficient, and he never broke a sweat doing it. When the song was over, his actions were always predictable. Whether he was indoors or outdoors, it was always the same move. His trademark grin would be transformed into a big Cheshire cat smile, and a big belly laugh would follow. It all communicated a single thought: "Look at me. I may not be the best dancer in the house, but I'm the one guy in here who's got his act together." Reginald Lewis was cultivating that image for himself. No one was ever going to mistake Reginald F. Lewis for Chuck Jackson, but it didn't matter. Making all of this even more extraordinary was the fact that Reginald could hardly have been considered a big R&B fan. His musical taste, while varied, centered mainly on Modern Jazz.

Back then, Reginald was a man of modest means. Those nights in the dormitory, watching him shuffle his feet to the sounds of Chuck Jackson's "Any Day Now," I couldn't help thinking, "If this guy ever got enough money to dress like Chuck Jackson, the rest of the world had better watch out."

It turned out I was right. Lucien Stoutt, who served as Reginald's butler and chauffeur before Lewis died, noted that Reginald's theory about cultivating the right look remained intact. His appearance was a critical part of his daily routine. His fashion requirements always included finely tailored suits with all the accoutrements of the impeccably well-dressed businessman. It was still about the look, but it was no longer simply a look to be admired by a group of giggling young girls hoping to gain a glance from a stage performer. As he grew older, it had become something more purposeful and more intentional. It was intended to make a powerful statement to other powerful people. The look, the stance, and the glance had become muted messages that even in their silence seemed to scream out loud for all to hear: "Take a close look, people. Someone very important has just walked into the room."

Chuck Jackson went on to record two back-to-back hits in 1961 and 1962. "I Don't Want To Cry" and "Any Day Now." His recording of "Any Day Now" was the only R&B recording I ever recall Reginald reacting to this way.

CHAPTER 5:

THE ROAD TO VIRGINIA STATE

---

*"The single biggest problem with communication
is the illusion that it has taken place."*
George Bernard Shaw

The middle of August of 1961 had finally arrived. Once again I had to deal with a host of mixed emotions. In a matter of days, I would be leaving Baltimore and heading to Petersburg, Virginia, for the start of pre-season football practice. I was excited about starting my first year at Virginia State, but I also regretted having to leave family and friends behind. A few days earlier, my mom had accompanied me to pick out a nice footlocker. My older brother Clarence, a former military policeman, had convinced me that I needed a footlocker to secure my personal belongings. The two of us, along with my youngest brother, Tony, had already packed it up and taken it to the Camden railroad station (the current site of Oriole Stadium at Camden Yards) to have it shipped prior to my departure.

I had not yet determined how I was going to get to Virginia State. My dad worked as a longshoreman, loading and unloading ships in what is now Baltimore's inner harbor. Most of those ships were transporting grain shipments overseas. This meant that much of his work was seasonal, and the summers were always slow. While he had agreed to take a day off and drive me to campus, I was reluctant to have him do so. As slow as work was in the summer, I knew it would hit the family hard.

I determined that once I shipped my footlocker, I was going to find a way to get to Virginia State on my own. With a few dollars in my pocket from my summer job, I figured I would catch the Greyhound or Trailways bus to Petersburg. I wasn't sure how the other guys were going to get there, and I didn't ask them. I thought doing so would mean having to reveal my own financial insecurities.

Reginald and I were walking off the field at Bloomingdale Park after having finished our last neighborhood football
workout. He stopped and asked if I knew how I was going to
get to Petersburg. I said I wasn't sure but that I would likely
end up taking the bus. He said, "Why don't you ride down
with Butch and me?" Butch was his stepfather, Jean Fugett Sr.
I paused as if having to ponder all my many options and then
replied yes. Reg had no way of knowing it, but deep down, my
answer held more jubilation than was evident. It was more
than just yes. It was hell yes! He had just taken a tremendous
weight off my shoulders.

The day of our trip to Virginia State began in the early
morning hours. I had said my goodbyes to all my family,
friends, and my girlfriend the night before. The morning sun
was barely visible over the horizon as daybreak was nearing.
Now, I was standing on the porch with my mom waiting for
Jean Fugett Sr. to arrive. Up until this point, I had traveled
very little. Leaving home was a new and somewhat discom-
forting experience for me. Even though I had never thought
of myself as a Momma's boy, I was feeling a deep sadness at
having to leave my mom standing on that porch. Money was
always tight, but somehow she had found a way to come up
with a few extra dollars for me. Along with it came her typical
admonition for all five of her sons: "You make sure you give
this money to Mr. Fugett. When you ride in someone else's
car, you always chip in on the gas. This is gas money." Alice
Hart always made a point of saying, "I don't want any of my
boys to be moochers." Moochers were people who would ride
and not offer to pay for gas.

Before long, Butch and Reginald were pulling up to the curb outside of my house. Armed with this bit of motherly wisdom on gas money, I hustled down the steps and into the back seat of the car. I was now on my way to Virginia State, but there was one little problem. Neither Butch nor Reginald would accept the gas money. They both refused to allow me to carry out my appointed task. Admittedly, given the poor state of my finances, I did not put up much of an argument on this point. However, like a good son, I did tell my mom I made the offer.

Jean Fugett Sr. Makes a Lasting Impression

My dad, Willie Hart, was one of the finest men I ever knew. He was a hard worker and a great father to his five sons. Like most black men of his generation, he had experienced his share of highs and lows, but through it all he was always there for our family. He worked every day there was work to be done. When he passed away, he was nearly 95 years old. He was a good guy, but you always knew there was a clear line of demarcation between parent and child. It wasn't as if we couldn't speak with him, but I can't recall very many moments when my dad and I just sat around talking like a couple of regular guys.

I had met Reginald's stepfather, Jean Fugett Sr., previously, but until this trip I had not spent much time in his presence. I had no idea how this long trip was going to unfold, and I was beginning to feel the usual teenage tension that comes with meeting an older person for the first time. My first observation was that Butch, as Reginald affectionately called him, was a big man. He was tall, with broad shoulders and the body frame of a football lineman. I was immediately impressed with how friendly he was. He was a soft-spoken gentleman with a disarming smile that made him easy to talk to. I could see that he and Reginald hit it off well. They seemed more like big brother and little brother than stepson and stepfather.

Before long, the atmosphere in the car was alive with interesting conversation. When the subject got round to football, Butch spoke like a coach. He had lots of ideas about the game, which he shared freely. He seemed to know plenty about the CIAA (Central Interscholastic Athletic Association) football conference. Reginald and I would be playing in the CIAA for the next four years. I listened intently as he spoke about some of the great teams of the 40s and 50s. At some point during the conversation, I thought, "This guy sure knows a lot about CIAA football." Shortly afterwards it became clear why. Butch had played in the CIAA as a member of those great Morgan State teams in the early 1950s.

As the miles piled up along our journey, I began to feel more at ease and started to really enjoy the trip. It was beginning to feel like a bunch of young guys taking a road trip together. All of this was a new experience for me. Listening to Reginald and Butch going on and on, I began to get a sense of the special relationship that existed between the two of them. As the years passed by and I got to know Butch better, I was even more impressed with the nature of this fine gentleman.

With all of our back-and-forth banter, the time passed very quickly. Before we knew it, Butch, with a firm hand on the steering wheel, had the car on a slow glide path up the hill towards Williams Hall, the freshman dormitory. We had finally arrived on Virginia State's campus. This had been a great road trip. Our lives as college students and athletes were just beginning. Reg and I were both excited over the prospect of what lay ahead.

This Place Is for Those Who Have Come to Learn

Virginia State University was founded in 1882 as the Virginia Normal and Collegiate Institute, making it the first fully state-supported, four-year institution of higher learning for blacks in America. When Reginald and I arrived there in 1961, it was known as Virginia State College. Today, it's one of Virginia's two remaining land-grant institutions. I knew little about Virginia State before enrolling there. What little I did know had come from an occasional sports article in the *Baltimore Afro American* newspaper. I had the pleasure of meeting the highly regarded *Afro American* sports editor of that time, Sam Lacy, during an interview. It was another of those cherished moments made even better by the fact that he recalled both Reginald and me from our high school days in Baltimore. I had also discussed Virginia State with my sister-in-law, Arnita. She had grown up in Petersburg and was a graduate of Virginia State. I used the photo in the school's catalog to help me form a mental picture of the campus. I recall looking at the photo and thinking what a change it was going to be for me, having to spend the next four years at a place that looked like this. It was a far cry from the streets of West Baltimore.

The campus sits high atop a rolling landscape overlooking the Appomattox River in the Chesterfield County village of Ettrick. Back then, the campus's main entrance was located at the foot of a steep hill, requiring the negotiation of a long, winding road to reach the top. As picturesque and as beautiful as was the sight of Virginia Hall perched atop that bluff, I always resented having to climb that hill. Not having a car meant I often had to make that climb on foot. During the years I spent there, life was quiet, serene, and peaceful. It was ideal for study. Looking back on it all, Virginia State College in 1961 was exactly where I needed to be.

The setting at Virginia State's campus was tranquil and far slower than I was used to back home in Baltimore. This was especially true of the front campus. This area lay just beyond the doors of Virginia Hall, the administrative building. At that time, it would have sounded rather strange, coming from me, but I always enjoyed the calming atmosphere that could be found there. For reasons I never quite understood, it was one of the least traveled areas on campus. I suspect it may have had something to do with a campus rule I had neglected to read. The absence of foot traffic and the well-spaced benches made the place the ideal setting for quiet contemplation or conversation. Approaching campus from the front campus side left you with an unmistakable message: "This is a place for those who have come to learn."

Did That Guy Just Say Cheeks?

From the very first moment we set foot on Virginia State's campus, Reginald was determined to assert himself. He often spoke of being the lead dog on the football team. As he would put it, being the lead dog put you in a position to wield influence and make decisions. He also knew that being the lead dog meant lots of respect and recognition, and that the air just ahead of your nose was always going to be as fresh as a daisy.

We had only been on campus for a couple of hours before we caught up with Al Banks. With Al in tow, we were now a threesome. We immediately set about to explore the campus and find our way around. The first order of business was to visit the stadium and get a feel for its layout. We also thought it would be a good idea to check out Foster Hall, the student union building. This time of the year, there weren't many students on campus, so we had the run of the place. Lunchtime was nearing, so we began to make our way back to the dining hall to join the other newly arrived freshmen football players for afternoon lunch.

As we were passing the old Daniel gymnasium on our way to the dining hall, we noticed a group of guys walking toward us. We just assumed they were football players because they were humongous. There were four or five of them, and they walked shoulder to shoulder as we approached them. I happened to notice that one guy was wearing an army fatigue jacket with cut-off fatigue pants as shorts. From about 50 yards away, I could see that one of his calves was nearly the size of both of mine. I remember thinking that this guy had to be one of our linemen. In those days, it was common to have Vietnam veterans returning to college on football scholarships to finish their education. I just assumed that this was his story too.

As we approached them, the guy in the fatigues casually acknowledged us and said," I understand you guys are from Baltimore." We nodded an approving yes, and in a half-joking manner I replied saying "Yeah. We're the Baltimore Guys. Where are you from?" He boomed out in a deep voice, "Yeah. I'm from Baltimore too." Reginald and I both looked at each other with a kind of puzzled look. I had checked with my high school football coach, Julian Dyke, and felt I knew everyone on the roster who was from Baltimore. I had no idea who this guy was. Coach Dyke had told me that Robert Anderson, a senior running back from Baltimore's Southern High School, was on the team. For a fleeting moment, I thought this guy might be Robert Anderson, but according to what I had been told by Coach Dyke, Robert Anderson was not a big guy. There was no way this guy could be Robert Anderson. He was too big.

The conversation that followed was brief, but as far as we were concerned, it moved both heaven and earth.

I can still see the glazed-over look that came over Reggie's face as this guy boomed out a second time, "What's up man? My name is Bobby Cheeks." We both stood staring as he extended his hand to shake ours. His hand seemed to be the size of a baseball catcher's mitt. I didn't know what Reg or Al were thinking, but I felt as if I was staring down the lens of a camera, filming a bad movie. I had already made a quick calculation of my chances of making the first team. In the few seconds it took my brain to calculate the answer I knew they were slim. At the same time, I had every reason to believe that Bobby Cheeks's chances of making the first team were excellent. Putting the pieces together, I was able to construct the nightmare scenario we had been running from since junior high school. It was the one where we get repeatedly run over by this freight train of a man during scrimmages. Bobby Cheeks had finally caught up with us.

Back then, unlike today, the fullback was a primary ball carrier. He was expected to punish the defense every time he got his hands on the ball. Cheeks was over six feet tall and weighed close to 260 lbs. He was built for the job. We would soon learn that he had not lost a step in speed, and his running style was as ferocious as ever.

Okay, at some point Reg and I accepted the idea that we would have to live with this bit of unfortunate luck. We knew we could take some consolation in knowing that Cheeks would be on our team when the real games started. We could delight in watching him punish the hell out of the opposition. This thought had just begun to lift our spirits when we were introduced to last year's starting fullback. He was now a senior and the presumptive starter going into our season. His name was Ernie "Big Money" Turner. I took one look at "Big Money" and thought, "Boy, are we having a bad day." Ernie was even bigger, and some would argue faster, than Cheeks. Since neither of us weighed more than 175 lbs., this was not a pleasant prospect. I stood there thinking that now we would have not one, but two of these monsters running loose during scrimmages. I was starting to feel like a human piñata.

As we made our way towards the dining hall for lunch, I began to reflect upon those conversations we had had during our summer workouts back at Bloomingdale Park in Baltimore. Reginald chimed in "Man! Bobby Cheeks was the one guy we were glad to have missed in high school, and now he shows up here." To make matters worse, our new head coach, Willie Lawson, had a reputation for conducting long practices with plenty of punishing, full-contact scrimmages.

Our offensive sets in those days usually included two halfbacks and a fullback on the field at all times. Seniors Sidney Swann and Robert Anderson had already nailed down the two halfback positions. We conceded that Ernie Turner would probably start the season as the number one fullback on the first team (red team). This meant that Cheeks would end up starting the season with the second team (blue team). I played cornerback on defense, and I was aware that if I made the blue team, Cheeks would be the defensive linebacker lined up on my side of the field. For the record, Bobby Cheeks was every bit as ornery on defense as he was when running with the football on offense.

With Swann and Anderson firmly entrenched as the starters in the backfield, my best option was to make that blue team. There was little question that the ideal position for me would be wearing a blue jersey and lining up in the same backfield with Bobby Cheeks. The one place I did not want to be was on the third string, the white team, or the fourth-string team. Landing there would have guaranteed me the unenviable task of having to try and corral both Turner and Cheeks as the two of them trampled defenders during those long, hot practice scrimmages. I was a decent defensive football player, but my thin frame and my mindless bravery would have made me the ideal carpet for Cheeks and Turner's size 15 cleated football shoes. As for Reginald, he hadn't yet reached a point where he could begin to envision such a scenario as this. In spite of his slow start, Reginald still had his sights set higher. As far as he was concerned, there still was no clear-cut winner for the starting quarterback slot, and he was still gunning for it.

Kay Really Gets Around

There were always very distinguishable differences in our view of campus life. From the very first day, Reginald began talking about areas of interest that would become his first forays into this new world. It was apparent that he had given serious thought to campus life and the total experience. For him, campus life included much more than just class work. It included the social life, the library, athletics, concerts, work, and women and of course, there were the fraternities. Reginald had given the complete palette of possibilities considerable thought. He had determined that he was going to enjoy campus life in every respect and from every angle.

On the other hand, I had a more limited set of objectives. It would boil down to two things: First, make the team, and second, remain eligible for next year. Anything else was of lesser consequence. Even though my goals were small in number, they represented a considerable turnaround for me. Just six months earlier, I had no intentions or plans to attend college. The prospect of a football scholarship had been lingering in the air for my entire senior year of high school, but I held out little hope of actually getting and accepting one. Going to college had always been a distant prospect for me, but now I had undergone this sudden and dramatic change. I had become a full-time college student with a range of challenges to consider.

As the main student body began arriving, I could not help but notice the uniformity that underscored campus life. It was the kind of uniformity that had little to do with rules and regulations. It was more about the feel and the tempo of the place. There were young men and women lining up in the dining hall and doing so in an orderly fashion. It seemed as though the students all trudged along at roughly the same pace, yet they seemed focused and intent on getting to class on time. I was surprised to find that I was enjoying being a part of all this.

In the midst of all this uniformity, there were some aspects of campus life that were clearly not uniform. Most notable among these were the fraternities and sororities. They were in constant campaign mode, seeking to establish their own unique identity. Their message was clear and consistent: "We are different, and we like it that way." These were organizations with deep roots and long histories. The fraternities—Kappas, Alphas, Omegas, and Sigmas—and the sororities—Deltas, AKAs, and Zetas—had long figured out how to mark their territories. Their unique insignias, ceremonies, songs, and rituals were well known throughout the campus community. The practice I found most intriguing was the organization's use of the Greek alphabet. The omnipresent caps, sweaters, and banners were always embellished with Greek letters. This made the entire fraternity and sorority scene rather ambiguous and confusing for me. Here, I'm about to admit to something that is likely to subject me to serious scrutiny and even ridicule. I would rather attribute it to the ignorance of my youth, but it does help make the point of just how unprepared I was for the college experience.

During the first couple of weeks of football practice, players made up most of the campus population. Most of the upper classmen on the team were fraternity men who took great pride in displaying their fraternity colors. The most visible of the paraphernalia were the caps with Greek letters on them. I had been a member of an unsanctioned high school fraternity, but the logic of using Greek letters was always a little puzzling to me. My understanding of fraternities and sororities had not fully evolved to the point of knowing the purpose of the Greek Alphabet. It was all a big mystery to me, and the curtain was just about to rise and reveal just how little I understood about college life.

Sometime during the first week, a group of us football players decided to take our own self-guided tour of the campus. Along the way, we met this young lady. Her name was Kay, and she was just a tad over five feet tall. She was well built, attractive, and blessed with a great personality. It was easy to see she was a popular figure on Virginia State's campus. I made a mental note of this, thinking I would see her again.

As we were talking, it came to me that I had observed a lot of guys walking around the campus wearing red and white golf caps with the letters KAΨ on the front. I thought to myself, maybe Kay was a homecoming queen or last year's Miss Virginia State. As we were parting ways with Kay, I turned and without so much as an afterthought whispered to Reginald, "Man that chick Kay sure does get around. Have you noticed how many guys are walking around the campus with her name on their caps." He looked at me with this incredulous expression and said, "Hart, you have to be joking. Don't you know that those letters stand for Kappa Alpha Psi?" I actually said it in a half-joking manner, but in truth I was far from certain about the connection between Kay's name, the fraternity and those caps. Reg could hardly stop himself from laughing. Before it was all over, even I was laughing. When the dust had finally settled, I thought to myself, "Hell, this was another piece of valuable learning. Better to make the faux pas with Reginald than with some group of guys I didn't know." As we had done in the past, when it was all over, we moved on to the next thing.

Throughout the summer, Reginald had talked about becoming a fraternity man. I was never certain if he had come to college with a predisposition for a particular fraternity, but he quickly became enchanted with the idea of becoming a Kappa. By the end of our first year, I had come to the same conclusion. There were a large number of Kappas on the football team our freshman year. Most were starters. Some were colorful, and all were fiercely loyal to their fraternity. With the exception of hard drinking, they also had social values that I could easily identify with. When Al Banks indicated he was also planning to pledge Kappa, the die had been cast. The Baltimore guys were all going to pledge Kappa.

As the year progressed, Reginald's desire to pledge Kappa became an obsession. He felt the other fraternities were cool, but the Kappas had their own brand of cool. To listen to Reginald, there were two upperclassmen who had really impressed him. They were Harold Amaker and James Drewery. Both guys were Kappas. Reginald thought they were everything a Kappa was supposed to be.

Reg had gotten it into his head that Amaker and Drewery had it all figured out. He would go on at great length, talking about how they had their stuff together. Neither of them seemed to require a lot of attention, and according to Reg, he could tell that both were doing just fine, in every aspect of campus life. In his opinion, they were good students, good-looking guys who appealed to the ladies, and they both seemed to be in total control of their personal business. Whether any of this was true or not didn't seem to matter to him, he was sold on these two guys.

What was most important to Reginald was the fact that these two guys always left you wondering what they were up to. Before long, the decision had been made. Once he became a Kappa, Amaker and Drewry would serve as his new role models. Since he was never one to tell, it would always be left to others to try to figure out what Reginald Lewis was up to.

I mentioned this to Amaker many years later, and he just laughed, saying, "I never knew I had that kind of effect on Reginald."

Closing The Gap

Things were coming at us fast, and I hadn't prepared well for the sensory overload. Reginald was fairing a little better than I was. He was confident, which meant he was making good use of his commanding presence when he was on the practice field. Yet, there remained something I had noticed during our practice sessions earlier in Baltimore. His passes still lacked velocity, and the crispness in his throws that I had once seen was still absent. We were both having problems trying to perform at levels we had become accustomed to. At some point, I started to feel overwhelmed. Whatever special status we carried at our high schools was gone as the coaches began ramping up both the pace and their expectations.

In the middle of all of this came the usual hazing experience, which I had anticipated. Every freshman felt the weight of having to be submissive to the upper classmen on the team, but this was especially tough for Reginald. He hadn't yet disconnected from his Dunbar experience, where he was treated as someone special. Having to endure this level of physical and mental humiliation weighed heavily on him. He hated every minute of it and would rail on at great length about how unfair it was, having to endure this kind of "chicken crap." Especially since it was coming from a few guys he felt weren't as talented as he was. He referred to them as guys who weren't good enough to carry his jock strap.

In this, he may have been right, but I saw it as something to be endured. It was a ritual that everyone had to go through. Reginald viewed it as an unacceptable kind of debasement that did nothing to improve the team and did everything to give a bunch of guys the right to pound the hell out of us. As much as he wanted to protest, he finally decided that discretion was the better part of valor, and it would be best to keep his head down until it was all over. The good news for us was that the actual hazing period was brief.

Leading up to this point, I had spent little time thinking of going to college as anything more than having another opportunity to play football. I had always had good grades in school, but to be completely honest about it, I had coasted through my last few years. Now, I was totally consumed with the thought of making the team, but the importance of grades was not lost on me. I was still determined to keep my grades up, but I felt I needed to be strategic in college. The strategy was simple, do whatever it took to keep my football scholarship and my eligibility; nothing more, nothing less. Of course, there was the pride factor at work, which had always served as my safety valve. I had determined that there was no way I was going to flunk out of Virginia State, that year or any other year.

Reginald and I both wanted to become stars on the football field, but beyond that, his portfolio of goals had much more depth than mine. It didn't take me long to figure out that he had put much more thought into preparing for college than I had. For example, he had a better handle on what his major was going to be and what courses he was going to take his freshman year. He'd perused the catalog and was already laying out plans for courses in his sophomore year. More important, he had actually considered the prospect of graduating one day and starting a career. In this respect, being holed up with guys like Reginald and Al Banks for four years was one of the best things that ever happened to me. It was exactly where I needed to be at that stage of my life and over time a more robust college career plan would begin to evolve for me.

Reginald was never bashful when it came to heaping praise upon Dunbar High School. He would go on and on about the academic superiority of the Dunbar graduate over other Baltimore public school graduates. There was little question that he was proud of his school, but in listening to him I had the feeling he had sized me up as a pretty good football player but not much of a student. I may have contributed to this perception by revealing that I had enrolled in a non-college prep curriculum in high school. Even so, I never doubted my ability to do well in the classroom if I had to. I just never saw the need to go all out, because I could coast in my classes and still maintain the grades required to participate in sports.

I had clearly fallen into the trap of setting low expectations for myself. I was also great at finding excuses. I recall wondering why I should bust my butt when I could see no way of coming up with the money to pay for college tuition. Another favorite thought was that a high school diploma would be good enough. Aside from my teachers, I had known only a few people who had actually graduated from college. An older guy in our neighborhood, Lorenzo Foy, was the one person my parents would often hold up as an example of someone who was going somewhere. Lorenzo had graduated from Morgan State College in the 50s.

One thing was for certain: Reginald Lewis did not lack for confidence. I found his seemingly endless supply of self-confidence to have been among his more appealing qualities. Others might disagree, but with the possible exception of his self-proclaimed sexual exploits, I never found him to be a boastful braggart. He was very opinionated and privately he thought highly of himself, but never a loudmouth braggart.

However, I would soon discover an aspect of his personality that would make him less endearing. Reginald always had his measuring stick out when it came to assessing other people. He had to know how they stacked up against his own measure of excellence. It included everything, from performance on the field, career choice, food, politics, and social awareness to grades. He always seemed to be in search of some attribute that he could use as a marker to measure himself against others. His need to do this seemed to matter most if you were a good friend or someone he liked. It was as if he was trying to determine whether a person was worth him investing any serious time with. In a casual conversation, he was always polite, but when it came to investing his time in a serious friendship, it was much different. If, in his mind, you were someone whose ideas were shallow or lacked substance, you might be met with a dismissive attitude.

Reginald was always willing to be a bit more flexible when it came to his relationships with athletes. A Jock could have been a "mental midget" in the classroom, but if he had demonstrated that he could totally dominate his opponent on the playing field, he was going to get an extra measure of respect from Reginald Lewis. If it happened that the athlete was the total package, meaning he was also proficient in the classroom, he would get an even greater level of respect from Reginald. Reg was a competitive guy, and this was just his competitive nature revealing itself.

A Moment of Mutual Respect

All incoming freshmen were required to take a battery of English and math proficiency tests before class started. These tests would determine a student's readiness for college-level math and English. We all knew these tests would be quite comprehensive and very demanding. For years, passing them had been a major hurdle for freshman football players. The routine had been that a large number of them would fail one or both tests. This meant they would be required to take remedial English or remedial math or, worse yet, both. These were non-credit courses.

There were the pre-test pep talks by head football coach, Willie Lawson, encouraging every player to do his absolute best, but you could hear in his voice that he had just about conceded that our group would be no different than previous freshmen classes.

When the day of reckoning arrived and all the test results were in Coach Lawson's hand, he stood before the entire team and began the dreaded process of informing players of their results. The final reading revealed he had been right. As in years past, some had failed both tests, and nearly everyone had failed one. However, there was a ray of good news.

Coach Lawson announced that this year, two freshmen players had passed both tests and they were both from Baltimore. I held my breath, thinking there were four of us from Baltimore: Robert Cheeks, Albert Banks, Reginald Lewis and me. I had known Al to be a good student and a smart guy. While Reginald and I had gone to different schools, I never doubted he was a smart guy. This process of elimination was made even tougher with the inclusion of returning Vietnam veteran Robert Cheeks. Two of my older cousins, Harold Hart and Warren Edmonds had been athletes at Baltimore's Douglas High School when Cheeks was a student there. Despite his hulking physique, I had long ago heard that he had been a standout in the classroom. Cheeks was a smart guy, too.

I looked around the room, and there were no engaging stares coming my way from those guys. It was hot in the room, and I was starting to sweat bullets. To make matters worse, it seemed as though Coach Lawson was purposefully engaging in a form of Chinese water torture. His pre-announcement speech seemed endless and filled with everything but the names of the players who had passed both tests.

The tension had built to a point where I just could not take it anymore. Finally, I said to myself, "The hell with it, I don't care one way or the other." Just at that moment, Coach let go. He shouted out the names Robert Cheeks and Linwood Hart as the two freshmen who had passed both tests. I heaved a big sigh of relief. I had a good feeling after taking those tests, but this kind of high drama had left me drained. Still, I was happy.

I could see that Reg was visibly disappointed. Like every freshman on the team, he had hoped Coach Lawson would call his name, eliminating the need to take non-credit courses. I respected every guy in that room, so I did nothing to express my exhilaration, but it was one of the proudest moments of my life.

When we broke from the room and headed for the field, Reginald came up behind me and did something I was not expecting. He caught me by the arm and said, "Hey man, slow down. I just wanted to congratulate you on passing both tests. Those tests were not easy, and you nailed both of them." He then trotted ahead of me, making his way to the field. He was more than gracious in offering his congratulations. He even added that he was proud of me representing Baltimore in a positive light. It was the first time I had seen that side of Reginald Lewis. In the days ahead, we were destined to have our share of disagreements, but I have always believed that this was a significant moment for the two of us. Reginald never did put away his measuring stick, but it was the moment when mutual respect arrived for both of us.

CHAPTER 6:

ROOMMATES, CONVERSATION, AND MOM'S COOKING

"*Not everything that is faced can be changed, but nothing can be changed until it is faced.*"
James Baldwin

The prospect of having to choose a roommate was something I had given little thought to. When Al Banks and I realized we were both going to be teammates at Virginia State, it was just assumed that we would also be roommates. Neither of us had talked about it.

All first-year players had been instructed to report to the freshman dormitory, Williams Hall. The August heat in Virginia was stifling, and air-conditioning was not even an afterthought in those days. Williams Hall was a large building with long hallways. With the doors and windows open, and if you were lucky, you might catch an occasional and much appreciated breeze. For the two and a half weeks of pre-season football practice, Williams Hall would be home for the entire team. Freshman players were requested to line up in the lobby for room assignments. This was a fairly routine matter, as most of the upper classmen had already partnered up with their roommates from the previous year. Many were already in their rooms unpacking or visiting from room to room. Al, Reg, and I had already assumed our places in line together, without giving much thought to order. As we were nearing the desk where the sign-in would occur, I noticed Reginald step out from his position in line and move to the spot in front of me. I didn't think much of it at the time, but as we reached the sign-in desk, I realized we were positioned as the next twosome. One of the coaches had been placed at the head of the line to assist with the assignments. He pointed to Reg and me and said, "Okay. You two guys sign in here."

This wasn't a rigid process. I didn't feel as if I was not allowed an opportunity to make a change, but not wanting to make a choice between Al and Reginald had left me in an awkward position. Both were my friends, so I decided this was not the moment I needed to make a choice. I thought that the assignments would only be temporary. I figured there would be plenty of time to work this out before school started. Al was paired up with Kenny Moore, another freshman quarterback. When the time came to select roommates for the school year, everyone seemed okay with their arrangements. Reginald and I remained roommates, and so did Al and Kenny. The situation had resolved itself.

Sometime later, I recall asking Reginald about his maneuvering in the line to set up the circumstances of our becoming roommates. He stared at me with a look of feigned indignation and said, "Come on Hart, you know I wouldn't do anything like that." Reginald always denied he had done anything to set it up, but he always had a smile on his face when denying it. Actually, Al, Reginald, and I spent so much time together, it seemed the three of us were roommates anyway.

I have always considered this incident to have been instructive in understanding how Reginald dealt with things. Planning and timing were always a part of his thought process. At no time had he asked me to be his roommate. Never once did he give a clue that he had considered it. At some point, well in advance of us arriving on campus, I believe he made up his mind that if he had to have a roommate, it was not going to be a complete stranger. Better yet, if it could be someone he already knew and that someone happened to be a pass receiver on the football team. That would be just perfect. When the time came to act, he was unapologetic in making his move.

Time and time again, this same scenario would play itself out. He would determine what he wanted to do, well in advance of others. He would do little to telegraph his intentions, and when the time was right, he would make his move.

After our first month together, I was convinced that he would have preferred not having a roommate at all. He was overly protective of his space and secretive about everything. Reginald was deeply committed to maintaining certain boundaries, which was fine by me. In fact, our co-existence was made manageable because we had two qualities in common. We both wanted our space, and we were both close-mouthed about our personal matters.

Productive Conversation: What I Know Now but Didn't Know Then

The amazing thing about our ability to learn is that there are times when we are learning something of great value and we aren't even aware of it. Throughout this book, you will read about moments when Reginald and I had debates, disagreements, and arguments. Though many of them were heated, they never resulted in hard feelings or anger. Somehow, we always found a way to wrap it up and move on to the next thing. I have always believed that it was in those moments that I came to appreciate the value of a productive conversation. Without giving it much thought, I was learning how to disagree without becoming disagreeable.

In his book *Dialogue and The Art of Thinking Together,* published in 1999, author and MIT Professor William Isaacs describes the atmosphere for productive dialogue as resembling a container. He explains how it is possible to build strong relationships by first building strong containers in which to *sustain conversation.* He uses the analogy of a container, much like a cup or a bowl, in which we submit all of our views, opinions, and sometimes our feelings during a discussion or dialogue. When we engage others in this manner, what we say and how we say it becomes key in sustaining the relationship and the conversation. Knowing and trusting the other party beforehand is critical, because all that we say and do goes into our relationship container. If all parties agree that their stake in the relationship is too important to mess it up, there's a good possibility their containers can sustain a lot of heat.

Relationships that are not built this way cannot sustain honest disagreement, which means there is little chance of having a productive conversation. You cannot pour steaming hot liquid into a container made of paper and expect it to hold up. Conversely, you cannot expect to repeatedly pour "White Hot Rhetoric" into it and expect the relationship to last. In our case, there was much we disagreed on, but we were always able to set the container aside and let it cool off until the next engagement. It may not always have been civil discourse, but when it was over, we left it as friends.

It helps if all parties have an equal footing on the field of debate. I wasn't kidding myself; I always felt that if Reginald had the upper hand, those conversations wouldn't have been nearly as productive. Growing up in a house of five boys, it was not unusual for disagreements between me and one of my older, bigger brothers to end up in a wrestling match. Whenever that happened, I usually ended up losing. My brother would invariably have too much weight, too much power, and too much leverage. While Reginald and I both could be stubborn, neither of us had leverage over the other, and we were well past the point in our friendship where we felt the need to get physical over a disagreement. Some of our disagreements would go on well into the night without a sign that either of us was willing to yield. Whenever that happened, one of us would simply shut it down by saying to the other guy, "Okay, man. No hard feelings, but you need to take your ass to sleep." We discovered that we both liked to talk and we were both willing to be the audience for the other guy's speech.

As it turned out, Reginald was a good roommate and the walls that had existed early on would slowly come down. Years later, once we were adults, I recall him once asking me, half-kiddingly, if I would be interested in coming to work for him. I replied, "I don't think so. Why mess up a good friendship?"

The Scatter Rug

At first glance, it was hard to tell if Reginald was a person of means or if he was just another guy struggling to make it. I thought it rather peculiar that a guy from our neighborhood was showing up for college with his own table radio, a tape recorder, bathrobe, bedroom slippers, pajamas, and a complete shaving kit. These may not have been big things to most people, but I was really impressed. I was aware that he didn't live in a big house or have a ton of money, yet he always seemed to have whatever he needed. I had shown up with my small transistor radio and a beat-up desk lamp I had shared with my brother Rod. My sleepwear included a pair of flip-flops and a couple of pairs of shorts and tee shirts that I had on unofficial consignment from the school's athletic department.

Our room was small and confining, especially for two growing young men. After a bumpy start, we soon found out that if you really worked at it, you could make it work. Making it work meant we had to be flexible and open to accepting each other's peculiar quirks.

Reginald had a scatter rug that he placed in the middle of the floor, positioned ever so slightly so that it favored his side of the room. It soon became clear that this rug would serve as his territorial marker. Nothing was said, but the body language spoke volumes. Your stuff is on that side of the rug, and my stuff is on this side of the rug. This boundary would gradually come down later, but when we first settled in, the territory was marked by that rug, and I willingly acceded.

There were times when Reginald's fondness for that rug extended well beyond its use as territory marker. There were moments when it seemed to have the power of a magic carpet that could take him to some far-off place. This always seemed to happen when he was troubled or in need of a little warmth on those cold mornings and or late evenings in our dorm room.

Williams Hall, the freshman dorm, was built in 1935, and like most buildings of that time, it relied upon steam-generated heat. There was a single radiator in our room. It was close to the wall, positioned directly under the window. When the weather turned cold, its performance, at best, was hit and miss, meaning sometimes it worked, sometimes it didn't. What little heat it generated would usually escape through the window.

When it was really cold, Reginald would often sit on the edge of his bed with his feet and toes buried deep into the pile of his scatter rug. I always assumed he was thinking about his family and being back in Baltimore. Sitting there staring into space, with his arms folded and the comfort of that soft rug on his feet, he appeared unusually serene and totally at peace. For a guy who was usually going full blast, seeing him in this mood was a rare sight. Whenever it happened, he seemed to open up, telling funny stories about something that had happened to him growing up or sharing a story about his grandfather or another family member. These were rare moments for a guy who treasured his privacy. It would be the most relaxed I ever recalled seeing him. I never knew who sent him that rug, but I'm sure they had no idea how their gift had served Reginald.

Missing Mom's Home Cooking

When it came to eating in the campus dining hall, the food was okay, but it was never going to replace mom's home cooking. Reginald complained about every meal served in the dining hall. There was rarely anything that met his taste. Initially, I had very little compassion for him. I attributed his behavior to the posturing of a pampered guy who was used to getting everything his way at home. I had grown up with four brothers. Dinner was never a good time to be indecisive or choosy. Good manners were always enforced, but a moment's indecision or an innocent complaint could cost you that chicken leg or that last roll you may have been eyeing.

It wasn't long before I began to realize I had been wrong about Reg. He really did have a sensitive stomach. It was a condition that gave him problems whenever he ate certain foods, and these were items that frequently found their way onto the dining hall menu. I was beginning to wonder if he could survive the year without his mom's cooking. Sometimes, I tried to help him out by trading off my serving of things he found easier to eat. On those infrequent occasions when there was something on the menu he could eat, he would do just about anything to get an extra portion. Pulling it off would usually require him to be at his best. He would be wheeling and dealing to make a bad situation better.

I had started to build up my playing time on the football team, which meant I was no longer a stranger on campus. One result of this was a budding friendship with a young lady who worked in the cafeteria. Her name was Trudy and she was a junior. Trudy was tall, soft spoken, and attractive. Her southern drawl was so authentic, she seemed to be right out of central casting. I was always puzzled as to how I merited the favor of her affections, but it was not something I was going to spend a lot time trying to figure out. Among her many positive attributes, there was one that Reginald took special note of. Trudy worked on the serving line in the dining hall.

Trudy was an easy-going, pleasant person, but when she took her place on the dining hall serving line, something rather astonishing would happen. Her transformation was stunning. She quickly became a personality akin to Jerry Seinfeld's character "The Soup Nazi." She was stern and highly disciplined when it came to doling out measured proportions to students. Starving looks and wimpy complaints meant nothing to Trudy. Chicken one day, macaroni and cheese the next. She was focused like a laser, and if she didn't like someone, she could even be miserly.

I guess I could say I was the one exception. At least, if you had asked Reg, that's what he would have said. I never had to deal with this tough, snarly side of Trudy's personality. It was something she reserved for others. When it came to serving me, I always received more than generous portions of whatever she was serving for the day. Reginald, Al Banks, and I always ate together. Reginald quickly took notice of Trudy's bias and was quick to comment that my portions of whatever Trudy was serving were always humongous and eye-popping. While he was quick to voice his displeasure with this development, he was just as quick in concluding that, with my help, it could be the answer to his daily food dilemma.

Reginald was always a guy with a watchful eye for opportunity. In spite of his charge of unfairness, he saw Trudy as a potential solution to his dining hall problem. He proposed the idea that whenever the dining hall was serving something he liked, I could use my charm to get Trudy to boost my portion. If it was something a fellow worker was serving, he proposed that I use my charm to persuade her to reach over into the other server's pan and scoop out super-sized portions for me. I could then split my extras with him. By deploying this plan, he would just look to me to make sure Trudy did the right thing. I had some initial reluctance, but Reg insisted it would work because this young lady was head over heels about me. He was convinced she would do just about anything to make me happy. This was one of my earliest exposures to the persuasive qualities of Reginald Lewis. It worked. I agreed to give it a shot.

It didn't take long for me to discover that there had been a couple of big flaws in Reg's plan. The first flaw was there would rarely be anything on the dining hall menu that he liked.

The second flaw was in assuming that Trudy was going to be an easy mark for this scheme. The problem was, Trudy had one unbreakable rule, and it applied even to me. She was not going to schlep from one station to the next trying to get me extra stuff from the other servers. My humongous, eye-popping portions were limited only to the stuff she was assigned to serve that day. If she was serving something I didn't like or Reginald didn't like, that was too bad.

When I tried to encourage her to expand her reach into other areas of the serving line to help out Reginald, Trudy was having none of it. I soon found that her delightful southern drawl was merely a cover. Lady Trudy was no pushover. I lobbied hard on behalf of my friend, but the look on her face spoke volumes. I came within a whisker of losing her affections and my favored status in the dining hall line. For a guy with my frail 175 lb. frame, this I could not allow to happen. I needed the favored treatment if I was ever going to bulk up.

I called Reginald over and said, "My friend, you need a new game plan. This one was dead on arrival." He jokingly declared that I had shown myself to be less than a loyal friend. For Reginald, this had become a real John F. Kennedy moment: "Ask not what your roommate can do for you, but what you can do for your roommate."

This left Reginald on the horns of a dilemma, and he was not going to stop until he found a workable solution. After all, he was looking at spending the next four years on this campus. He would later resort to using his charm and guile on the other ladies in the serving line. When that failed, he came up with something more practical. He gradually began to take fewer meals in the campus dining hall. He became a regular patron at Phil's Grill, the little eatery at the bottom of the hill, near the campus. Phil's was a regular gathering spot for students looking for a change in their routine or a break from eating dining hall food. Like many students at Virginia State, Reginald did not have a lot of money, and he was not a guy to part with a dollar easily. I'm sure the extra expense of having to eat most of his meals off-campus put a crimp in his funds. However, he was a man in search of a meal that he could easily digest. Phil's was frequently the answer.

I never spent much time at Phil's. The establishment operated strictly on a cash basis, and cash was something I had very little of in those days. Besides, as a member of the football team, we ate well. Unlike Reginald, I never had trouble finding something on the dining hall menu that I liked.

At the start of my senior year, I began dating Frances Washington, a senior from Winchester, Virginia. She and her sister Harriet were regular patrons of Phil's. They would occasionally, bump into Reginald while he was having a meal there. They became friends with Reginald. When I began dating Frances, Reg took it upon himself to become her biggest promoter, trying to convince me that we would make a great couple. It would later lead to him playing a humorous, yet meaningful, role in our decision to get married.

CHAPTER 7:

THE HARD KNOCKS OF MAKING THE TEAM

"Three things can happen when you throw the ball, and two of them are bad."
Darrell Royal (University of Texas)

The late summer heat in Petersburg, Virginia, was stifling. Unfortunately for Reginald and me, our days were about to get longer and hotter. Coach Willie Lawson had acquired a reputation for running physical two-a-day practices in the sweltering heat. There would be lots of scrimmaging and live contact. He had no way of knowing it at the time, but it would end up being especially tough on the new crop of freshmen quarterbacks.

Reginald had often spoken of last year's quarterback, Dewayne Jeter as the guy he wanted most to be like. Jeter had finished his eligibility the previous season but was returning to serve as the quarterbacks coach. During his four-year career at Virginia State, Jeter had established himself as the premier quarterback in the conference. For the returning players, who had been his teammates during those years, his status was bordering on legendary. The search to find his successor was about to get under way in earnest. Reginald Lewis, Al Banks, or someone in the incoming class would be expected to demonstrate that they were capable of stepping into Jeter's rather substantial shoes. The fact that Jeter himself would be filling out the scorecard and evaluating each player's performance should have represented additional pressure for players auditioning for the job. This was not the case with Reginald.

It was early in the season and Reginald's confidence was without limits. When he found out that Jeter would be coaching quarterbacks, the prospect of being able to play under his tutelage was irresistible. He could hardly contain himself. Reg was certain that his take-charge style and exceptional quarterbacking skills would simply dazzle and amaze this campus legend. There was no way he could have known it at the time, but Dewayne Jeter was about to become a central figure in his football life and it was not going to be a pretty picture.

Reginald's unresolved throwing problems continued to plague him. It was something that Jeter was quick to notice. Reg soon discovered that Jeter was not easily impressed. He was also beginning to realize that Jeter could be an especially tough coach. The lack of stellar evaluations coming from Jeter was causing Reginald to have renewed feelings about his once-admired hero. Still, he did not kid himself. He knew he was not performing at the top of his game, but he would often claim that Jeter was being unusually harsh in his critique of him. We both acknowledged that Jeter's record of athletic accomplishment gave him plenty of room to criticize poor performance on the field.

In conversations with Jeter prior to writing this book, he said, "I had very little knowledge of Reginald Lewis before he showed up at Virginia State. I always liked his confident, feisty manner as a young quarterback, but he never demonstrated much ability as a passer." Every day it was becoming evident that Reginald was not emerging as Jeter's #1 guy. It was also becoming just as clear that if he was going to see any playing time at all, he would have to turn things around in a hurry.

The situation was not much better for me. I was working out with the running backs, and I was having to struggle to keep up. Freshman football players are never going to receive a lot of nurturing on the field, so the answer for us was to suck it up and keep trying to find our game. Still, there was no denying it, the pressure of trying to perform and failing was beginning to mount on both of us.

The blistering Virginia heat was also beginning to take its toll. When we first arrived, I felt I was in the best shape of my life. Now, the rigors of two-a-day football practice was beginning to leave both of us drained and exhausted. The high point of the day was the much-anticipated lunch break. Following lunch, we had a chance to catch a two-hour rest in our dorm room before having to take that long walk back to the practice field. Having this free time to crash and think gave us a chance to console each other. The sounds of Jerry Butler's "Moon River" wafting through the hallways of Williams Hall always made consoling each other a whole lot easier. The calming and soulful sounds were courtesy of "Big" Joe Golden and his always-on 78 rpm record player.

Joe was a big music lover, and having our room within earshot of his was a blessing we had not counted on. Not only were we near Joe's music, we were also on the shady side of Williams Hall. Whenever we stretched out on our bunks, there was always the faint possibility we could catch a cool breeze coming through the screen in the open window.

Joe was a big, broad-chested senior lineman from Pittsburg, Pennsylvania. He may not have been our best lineman, but on the field he had a huge presence because of his size. Joe used his bulk well, meaning he gave up ground grudgingly. Off the field, he was blessed with a big heart and a great temperament. The thing I remember most about him was that he had a compassionate spot in his heart for the freshman players. During those mid-day breaks, Joe could be found roaming the hallways drinking iced tea and seeking a brief respite from the oppressive heat. Air-conditioning and Gator Aid had not yet made it to Virginia State.

Joe always made it his business to stop by our room and offer a few kind words of encouragement before continuing on his way. It was usually enough to lift our spirits and get us back in the right state of mind as we prepared for the afternoon practice. "Big" Joe Golden passed away years ago, but to this day, whenever I hear Jerry Butler's "Moon River," I think about Joe.

As is often the case with highly successful quarterbacks, Reg had been used to a different kind of treatment at Dunbar High School. Now that he was working under the close tutelage of Jeter, this was not happening. From the start of training camp, it was clear that the head football coach, Willie Lawson, had given Jeter a free hand in working with the quarterbacks. You could hardly blame him for doing this. Jeter had been a high achiever his entire football career, and he did not get that way by settling for average. He was pushing the freshmen, just as he had pushed himself. Even though I questioned his approach, it was always clear that he was settling for nothing less than our best. Unfortunately, for reasons that still puzzle me to this day, his best was something Reginald was unable to give.

This was a problem that would continue to plague him throughout the season.

The training camp was becoming a real revelation for the both of us. I have a vivid memory of being on the short end of one of Jeter's scathing critiques. It was during one of the early summer practice sessions. The running backs were going through a series of technique drills. After one of my failed attempts to get it right, Jeter made a biting assessment of my skills as a running back. He declared, at the top of his voice, "If this guy is a running back, I'm a lineman." I am certain Jeter does not recall that moment, but it was something I never forgot. I did not think much of him or his statement when he said it, but saying it when he did may have been one of the best things that could have happened to me. He was right, I was not performing well, and he was simply acting as my mirror to the truth. Jeter's message was plain and unmistakable: "You can't get by on what you did in high school. Either you show me something today, or I'm moving on to the next guy." As harsh as it seemed at the time, his assessment of my performance was a slice of real-world truth. It would take a while longer, but in the final analysis I believe Reginald also came to the same conclusion.

We Finally Break Camp

At the start of the regular season, incoming freshman quarterbacks Al Banks, Reginald Lewis, and Kenny Moore, a freshman from Farrell, Pennsylvania, had survived. They were the future hope for Virginia State's football fortunes. Harry Johnson, a very likable returning senior, and sophomore Spencer Rice were the returning veterans. I had a particular liking for Harry because he was from Danville, Virginia. Unknown to most of my friends, I was born in Danville, Virginia. It didn't matter to me that my family had left Danville when I was 8 months old. I always liked the idea of being able to claim more than one hometown. I had only been to Danville once since my family left. It was for a five-day visit with my cousins. Harry Johnson was a very likable guy, and to this day I have always thought of him as my homeboy.

My first impression of Harry Johnson was that, while he seemed capable, I thought both Reginald and Al possessed the natural tools to overtake him in the quarterback position. Harry was not a particularly big guy, and he had an average arm. However, Harry was a competitor, and he was not going to give up his job easily. If one of the new guys wanted his spot, they were going to have to wrestle it from his vice-like grip.

During the first couple of weeks of the regular season, Reginald seemed to have adjusted to his bumpy start. His passing form was still missing, but his attitude and his cockiness were returning. Reg always talked a good game, and he looked like a football player in his uniform. I liked this about him too. I always believed that if you are going to play the part, then you had damn well better look the part. When Reginald put on his football uniform, everything was always neat and in place. While being interviewed for this book,

Jeter said, "I did like the fact that Reggie was feisty. He kinda reminded me of myself." I thought, "Now, there is some consolation for Reggie."

It was becoming evident that freshman Kenny Moore was emerging as the leading contender among the freshman quarterbacks. In spite of his difficulties, when the regular season began, Reginald was taking some reps with the second squad. As the weeks wore on, his difficulties continued, and he began sliding further down the depth chart. This was not good news. Al was also fighting to stay off the third- or fourth-string team. They were both aware that continuing to fall further would mean being regularly served up on a platter to the first- and second-string teams. By now, I had moved into a spot in the second team backfield, alongside the considerably talented and equally menacing Bobby Cheeks.

I always liked Coach Lawson, but I never liked having to watch Reginald or Al being thrown to the wolves. They were my friends, and this was not what any of us had expected. As a running back and a receiver, I could understand and accept the need for live contact during practice. What I could never understand was why we subjected our young freshman quarterbacks to so much brutality that year. I kept waiting for the real Reginald Lewis to show up. Where was the guy with the rifle arm? Meanwhile, Coach Lawson was starting to increase the level of live contact. This meant more live scrimmaging and tackling under the stifling Virginia sun. The sun was just as merciless as the defenders facing Reginald.

Coach Lawson was not completely reckless, but there were times when I felt he had come really close. The #1 (red team) and the #2 (blue team) quarterbacks were often granted prima donna status, meaning rushing linemen were not allowed to hit them. However, if you were the quarterback on the third or fourth team, you were frequently exposed to the onrushing fury of defensive linemen. These guys were all determined to make a name for themselves at the expense of a poorly protected quarterback.

Getting Some Playing Time

By mid-season, the trend line for Reginald's football career was still falling, but he was still giving it his best shot. Earlier in the season, he actually got some playing time. I recall him entering the game with instructions to run a set series of plays. I was in the huddle at the time.

When Reg entered the huddle, he was so excited he could hardly restrain his youthful enthusiasm. This was going to be his big moment. This was going to be the moment his journey to the top would begin. He looked great and he sounded confident as hell. You could see in his eyes that he liked the idea of finally becoming the "Lead Dog." He quickly called the players together in the huddle and admonished a couple of them for their lack of attention. In an attempt to gain control of the huddle, he shouted out, "Listen up! Listen up, gang!" He was quickly reminded of his freshman status. Senior running back Ernie "Money" Turner fired back in an unusually stern voice, "Hey man, this ain't no gang you're running out here. This is a football team."

The look that came over Reggie's face said it all. He was not expecting to be lectured at such a moment. Still, he quickly settled down and ran an impressive series of plays, none of which were passes. I thought he performed well before being taken out. Neither of us knew it at the time, but that series was the most football he would ever play during his time at Virginia State. However, there did occur a point during that same game when I was able to see another side of Reginald Lewis. It was a less cocky, less freewheeling side.

Things were not going well for Reginald, but there was a play in the game where I caught a break. The events that followed that play served as another of those moments when we both found something to smile about. The play occurred on the opening kickoff of the second half. Defensive coach Hulon Willis had taken notice of my willingness to tackle during practice, so he decided that he wanted me on the field during kickoffs. I was assigned the position of "Gunner" on the opening kickoff. The gunner's job is to race downfield at top speed, seek out the ball carrier, and put him on the ground as quickly as possible. Fortunately for me, I was presented with a gift, as the guy who was assigned to block me fell down. This left me with a wide-open shot at the ball carrier, and I took it. It was the best tackle I ever made as a football player.

Reginald, who by his own admission was not a very good tackler, was impressed by the viciousness of the tackle. When

I returned to the bench, he gave me a look of approval, and with a big smile on his face he said, "Hart, you knocked the shit out of that guy." This was followed by a big hand slap and his trademark belly laugh. This was an indication of how he wanted to compete. He may have been struggling at the time, but Reg was a willing competitor, and he always wanted to be surrounded by people whom he considered tough and smart. He may not have been completely sold on the fact that I was smart, but because of that tackle he was willing to concede that I might have been tough.

We were now a couple of weeks into the season, and Reginald was beginning to slide further down the position chart. He frequently found himself quarterbacking the third-string team in practice, which meant he was being hit hard and being hit often. Reginald had been a starter throughout his high school career. This was a shockingly new experience for him. He was beginning to show the wear and tear from the battering he was taking in practice. He was always slow to rise whenever he was tackled or thrown to the ground by onrushing defensive lineman. I was certain this was one of the most humbling periods of his young life. He was now just a guy trying to get through a very tough slog. To his credit, he took the hits and carried on as best he could. The exceptional accuracy and arm strength I had witnessed in high school had simply vanished.

Reginald Lewis and Johnny Davis enjoy the campus view while sitting in Reginald's Austin Healey

Kappa Alpha Psi Chapter Officers pose for a photo on the steps of the Johnston Memorial Library. Left to right. Edmund Fields, Johnny Davis, Donald Muse, Reginald F. Lewis, Samuel Chisholm, Ivan Norrell, Lin Hart, Herman Bell.

Passing the time between classes. Left to right. Reginald Lewis, Edmund Fields, Lin Hart

Reginald Lewis (left) and Samuel Chisholm socializing with coeds outside Foster Hall.

Spring 1963 Kappa Alpha Psi Pledge Line.   Kneeling: Left to right. Lin Hart, Oscar Heyward, Ivan Norrell, Isadore Draper, Reginald Lewis, Sidney Allen. Standing: Left to right. Andrew Wills, Herman Bell, Samuel Banks, Bruce Smith, Frankie Boyd, Edmund Fields, Donald Muse, Johnny Davis.

Baltimore teammates. Kneeling, Reginald Lewis. Standing left to right, Albert Banks, Robert Cheeks, Lin Hart, Robert Anderson

Left to right. Herman Bell, Albert Banks. Election Day. Student council presidential candidate Albert Banks kidding around with campaign supporter Herman Bell.

Campaign manager Lin Hart, soliciting votes for his candidate, Al Banks, prior to the Student Council presidential election.

Reginald and my wife Frances, posing for a snapshot at our apartment. Reginald was paying us a visit, during his 1966 Christmas break between classes at Harvard.

Reginald joining me for a holiday toast in 1966. My glass contained orange juice. I'm not sure what was in Reginald's glass, but I'm fairly certain it was not orange juice.

Enjoying a moment, in the Hampton's, posing along side Reginald's prized Bentley. This photo was taken in 2011. Left to right Loida Lewis, Reginald's wife, Lin Hart, Frances Hart.

CHAPTER 8:

BALTIMORE GUYS—BREAKUPS AND BRAGGING RIGHTS

*"Acknowledge your weakness and surround yourself
with others for whom your weakness is their strength."*
Lin Hart

Baltimore's location by the Mason-Dixon Line had always been the spark for debates going back to well before the civil war. Was it in the north or was it in the south? I had grown up with the need to feel as though I was from the north and that Baltimore was in the north. Now that other students on campus began recognizing us as the Baltimore Guys, the sound of the word Baltimore had a nice ring to it

That famous marker, the Mason-Dixon Line is universally accepted as the borderline between the southern and northern states. The location of Baltimore, Maryland, relative to the Mason-Dixon Line was hardly a matter of ambiguity for us. For us, our hometown was situated squarely on the Mason-Dixon Line. That meant the city of Baltimore was to be counted among the bustling, urban centers of the north. While Baltimore was a large city, it was not to be confused with New York, Chicago, or Detroit. Our perception of being from some place similar was an inaccurate perception, but it was a perception that I had grown to accept.

While it may have been a perception, it was no small matter for Reginald. He was quite passionate when it came to casting his lot with the big city image of Baltimore and, more specifically, East Baltimore. With his flag of loyalty firmly planted in East Baltimore soil, Reginald Lewis felt he could handle anything this little southern school, Virginia State, could ever throw at him.

Northern snobbishness was not rampant. It would be unfair to say that all the kids from the north felt this way. More important, it was never anything as sinister as the traditional forms of prejudice that existed in those days. In my own case, it was fostered by ignorance and the need to boost my own self-confidence. It seemed so much easier to convince myself that I had an edge if I could make the claim that I was from a big city up north.

For Reg it played out in a different way. It had more to do with his affinity for the big northern cities. From the first time I met him, it was evident that Reg had his sights set on the big city. If you were from Boston, Connecticut, New York, or New Jersey, you received a "cool" pass from Reginald, meaning you were deemed cool until proven otherwise. If a person was from a rural area, they were initially judged less cool. There were exceptions, but generally first impressions were based on where you were from.

It would be fair to say that any perceptions of superiority we held were quickly dashed the moment we stepped onto the playing field and into the classrooms with our peers from the south. It quickly became apparent that the best of the south could more than hold their own with their counterparts from the north.

Every day I spent on Virginia State's campus made it less plausible that there was any big city advantage in being from Baltimore. To have continued down that path would have required a level of hope and imagination that I was incapable of sustaining.

All Was Not So Great Back in Baltimore

When we left Baltimore in August of 1961, we felt the tug and pull of knowing that we were leaving a lot behind. It was going to be quite a while before we would see family, friends, and most important of all, our girlfriends. With all the big-city preening going on, we had failed to take notice of the very subtle shifts taking place down at the campus mailroom. We didn't know it at the time, but we were both about to be jack-hammered and the jack-hammer was coming from the north. It was coming from Baltimore. My twice-a-week letters from my girlfriend back home had slowed down to a trickle. It wasn't much better for Reginald. It was as if our girlfriends had suddenly come up with a bad case of arthritis in their writing hands. It all seems rather funny now, but back then it seemed like a series of seismic blows to our egos.

Four months later, we were returning home for the Christmas holidays. It was with some trepidation, because by then each of us realized we would be confronted with the reality of finding that our relationships with our girlfriends had fallen into varying levels of disrepair. My relationship with my girlfriend had already disintegrated, Al's was teetering on the brink of disaster, and Reginald was privately strategizing on how to keep his faltering relationship a secret from us. Of course, this was an exercise in futility. As his roommate, I was already aware that his relationship was perilously close to going in the tank too.

The fact that each of us could wield sharp tongues with stinging verbal barbs meant the humor in our respective calamities was not going to be lost. This was especially true for Reginald. It wasn't often on display outside of our dormitory room, but Reginald Lewis had a great sense of humor. He could needle with the best of them and he knew how to use his sharp wit to get in his licks during these "beat down" sessions.

When Al and Reginald found out I had broken up with my girlfriend, their response revealed the bizarre nature of the friendship that existed between the three of us. As tight as we were, everything was fair game when it came to teasing. The only exception was the "Dozens." Talking about the other guys' mothers was definitely off limits. We were just like most immature and thoughtless 17- to 18-year-old college freshmen, and there were times when we were just merciless. Being dumped by one's girlfriend provided a tantalizing playground for our fertile minds. When it was my time to feel the heat, Al and Reginald understood this well. In their view, I had been peppering the hell out of them with a steady stream of trash talking. Now it was time for a little payback, and for a period of several weeks they were both unrelenting in their playback of my "Dear John" letter.

I took it well, because I knew there was some civility in the process of beating you down when it involved a woman. The recipient always knew that just as quickly as the kidding had begun, it could dissipate when it became clear you had enough. Still, this was always a delicate dance, but it worked because you knew the other guys were your friends. In spite of the verbal beat down, you knew they were the only guys on that campus you could count on if you were ever in a tough spot.

Ultimately, fate was working against all three of us. In a short span of three months, both Al and Reg joined me on the shores of misery as their relationships with their girlfriends crumbled like sand castles at high tide. It was rough going for a while, but in the end this experience of shared misery helped tighten our bond. It was one more experience we had in common as "The Baltimore Guys." The aftermath had left the three of us in the exact same situation. Still, there was a silver lining in the end for us. As expressed by the familiar tag line in the Southwestern Airlines commercial, "You are now free to fly about the country." Having broken up with our girlfriends back home, we were suddenly free to fly about the campus, and we did.

Bragging Rights

There were times during that first year when our room in Williams Hall was like a blazing inferno. The intensity of debates would build to incredible levels. This was especially true whenever the subject of high school football would arise. We were both passionate about our high school's sports teams. It was during these frequent encounters that I came to realize just how dogged Reginald could be. Once he spotted a weakness in your argument, real or perceived, you were going to be in for a long and rough slog.

I would soon come to learn that while he had not yet become a lawyer, Reginald was well versed on the lawyerly ways to win an argument. He had already cultivated the basic principles of courtroom demeanor in his debating style. In law, they teach you that if you can win on the law, argue the law. If you can't win on the law, argue the facts. If you can't win on the facts, argue policy. If you can't win on policy, attack the credibility of the witness.

Young Reginald's interpretation of this time-tested tenet was, "If you can't win on the facts, argue on what you recall. If you can't win on what you can recall, argue against what the other guy can recall. If that doesn't work, discredit the other guy's memory, plant your banner firmly in the ground, and declare victory."

Reginald's ideal platform for debate was world affairs, politics, and sports. I preferred to dwell in the realm of human nature (why people do what they do), the history of war, and sports. Given both our stubborn tendencies, most of our debates were inconclusive and often left us both hanging. We rarely solved anything, and we would usually end in a silent agreement to disagree.

The best illustration of how this worked can be seen by a close examination of what ended up being our long-standing debate over which high schools were among Baltimore's elite when it came to football teams. When the debate began, it centered on our final year of high school football, 1960. This debate had been raging for most of the summer, and we had carried it over into our first college semester. Now that we were roommates, it gained even greater intensity. Reginald contended there were only a handful of teams that could claim a spot on this list. He saw Dunbar on the list, but he saw no place for my high school, Edmondson. Oh man, we were off to the races on this one.

I knew that without some constraints in place, this was going to be a debate in which Reginald could have history on his side. Paul Lawrence Dunbar High School, nicknamed the "Poets," had opened in 1918 as an elementary school, and by 1940 it was the city's second high school for African-Americans. With the school's long, storied reputation, Reginald had history and time on his side. Dunbar had also produced some outstanding athletic teams over those years. I continued to press the point that this argument was solely about our last year of high school football, 1960. I felt that if the argument was going to be about 1960, I was on firm ground making my case for including my high school. Of course, there was always the question of my high school's varsity classification. As a new entry into the public school varsity ranks and with a small male student population, we had landed in the B Division. Still, I felt our 1960 team was better than Dunbar's A Division entry.

In 1960, Edmondson high had smashed every opponent we had faced. We finished the season as the only undefeated team in the Maryland Scholastic Association (MSA), with a 9–0 record. Along the way, we had distinguished ourselves by beating formidable A Division teams as well as every B Division opponent. At the start of the 1960 season, we had played the previous year's A Division champs, Loyola High, to a 7–7 tie during a pre-season scrimmage. Loyola had repeated as A Division champions in 1960. Dunbar had lost to Loyola 38 to 16, and they had won fewer than half of their A Division games in 1960. Our record in 1960 spoke for itself. We had defeated City High School, a perennial Baltimore high school powerhouse. Along the way, we had also defeated a tough Bel Air High School and ended their 18 game winning streak. We were 9-0. You would have thought this debate was over, but it was not going to end there as long as Reginald Lewis had anything to say about it.

As the debate was winding down for the evening, I causally threw in the fact that we had also won four straight games to begin our first varsity year in 1959. Here is where I learned a valuable lesson in debating with the Reginald Lewis. By bringing up 1959, I made a critical over-reach, which he quickly seized upon, and he never let go.

Reginald claimed that since I tossed in this comment about our 1959 record, I had opened up the discussion to include that year. On that basis, he claimed it would now be fair to include head-to-head varsity football competition between our two schools. It had only occurred once, and it happened in 1959. We both knew it was a game he was not likely to have forgotten. I objected, claiming our dispute was limited to the dispute over which school had the best team in 1960. Furthermore, I argued that Dunbar's mediocre record in 1960 made his attempt to include 1959 both capricious and argumentative. Well, that was not exactly what I said, but you get the point. In this instance, the budding lawyer in Reginald would have none of it. He powered ahead, giving little thought or importance to the source of our original dispute, Dunbar's mediocre record in 1960. At that point, I found myself asking, "How in the heck did I get here?"

Throughout high school, I had kept a scrapbook with a very detailed account and newspaper clippings of every game I had ever played in. During our summer workouts, I had casually mentioned this to Reginald. Recalling this, he insisted that I produce my scrapbook so he could find the information he needed to resolve this issue. Having put the entire debate behind me at this point, I allowed him to retrieve my scrapbook.

At this point I was thinking, "Man! I thought I could be stubborn, but Reg is even more stubborn than I am." He was determined to make this debate about 1959 and not about 1960. There was something buried deep in his memory, and I knew what it was. With a mischievous grin on his face, he hurriedly thumbed his way through the pages. He was searching for the one small piece of evidence he was certain would make his case. When he found what he was looking for, he shouted, "There, take a look at that." For him, the case was now closed. He had landed on the single article that would be the basis of his argument for the rest of our lives. Bragging rights over who had the best team had now been established. The dateline was October 24, 1959. The headline read, "Dunbar Tops Edmondson 20 to 0."

Just for good measure, he could not resist directing my attention to his favorite part of the article. It was that third paragraph and it read, "Dunbar added six more points in the second quarter, when Reginald Lewis fired a 27-yard touchdown strike to end William Tinkler." This was followed by his trademark belly laugh, which was so funny I could never resist joining in. This entire scene was just too funny to resist. We both cracked up laughing.

This was Reginald's coup de grace. It was his way of saying "Case closed. You lose. I win." In one fell swoop, at least in his mind, he had shifted the argument from who had the best team in 1960 to who had the best team throughout the four years of high school. I said, "You can't be serious. We were talking about 1960. That game was played in 1959." He countered with, "Yes, I know, but it really was about who had the best team, and since we beat you guys in the only head-to-head competition, I win." As hard as I tried, I could never move the argument back to the 1960 season.

This became a running debate that lasted the entire time we were at Virginia State and well into our later years. I never yielded my point, and as you might suspect, he never yielded on his. I would later take to calling this his Bragging Rights Game.

Say what you will, Reginald Lewis was tenacious, and he always gave himself high marks when it came to maneuvering a debate or a dispute into a direction that most favored him. While this may not have been his most skillful effort, it was typical of many debates we would eventually have. Like all those that came after this one, they usually ended with us both claiming victory and moving on to whatever was next.

The Guy Really Could Play

The year was 1959, and the two-year-old Edmondson High School had just won its first four football games of its inaugural varsity season. As the season wore on, we began to lose some of our momentum, and we entered the back half of the season with a couple of losses. We were getting ready to square off against Dunbar High's vaunted "Poets." It was a home game for us, and Dunbar was in the midst of another winning season. It was a perfect day for football, and the stands were full of students eagerly awaiting the arrival of Dunbar. Game day at our stadium always got me fired up. The sensory effect of seeing the playing field and the stands ablaze with our school colors—scarlet red, and white—always got my heart pumping and the adrenalin flowing. Looking up into the stands, the cool blue sky served as the perfect backdrop for the perfect day.

The bright yellow visitors' school bus had slowly pulled into the school's parking lot, on the hill high above the football field. The Dunbar "Poets" had finally arrived. As they got off their bus, their brightly colored gold and maroon uniforms gave them a menacing yet professional appearance. They looked formidable. Dunbar's discipline and businesslike approach was on full display as the players formed a perfect line that slowly snaked down the long winding stairs leading to the entrance gate to the field just below them.

As I watched them descend those stairs, I found myself caught up in a moment of conflicting emotions. I had never attended Dunbar, but as a kid growing up in Baltimore city, I had grown to respect those colors. Seeing them in this light conjured up memories of how Dunbar and their coach, Bill "Sugar" Cain, had so magnificently represented Baltimore's black community in those early years following public school integration in 1954. With Coach Cain at the helm, Dunbar had taken on the city's white high school powerhouse teams and distinguished themselves by winning a string of citywide championships. For many of the city's African-American population, Dunbar's maroon and gold had served as a banner of black respect in Baltimore.

My emotional conflict was fleeting and momentary. It quickly evaporated when the Dunbar Poets filed through that gate past us and onto the field. Their "no-nonsense, all-business" demeanor made an instant impression upon me. These guys were serious about the business at hand, and this game was going to be a dogfight. This was the slap to the side of the head that I needed. It jolted me back into my current reality. I would have to put that banner of black respect aside for a while. The time had come for me and my teammates, both black and white, to strap up and get ready for a dogfight. These Poets had not traveled all the way across town to recite poetry. They had come to kick some butt, and we didn't want it to be ours.

Just at that moment, I caught Reginald out of the corner of my eye. As he jogged past me, we made brief eye contact. With a polite nod of the heads and a barely audible exchange, we acknowledged each other. That was it. It was time to get it on.

Reginald Lewis was the starting quarterback for Dunbar that afternoon. I came in direct contact with Reginald twice during the game, both times on rushes from my position as a defensive end. No words were exchanged. In the end there was not very much to talk about. It was all business from start to finish. Dunbar won the game convincingly. The final score was Dunbar High 20, Edmondson High 0.

I was on the field for every play that day and can attest to the fact that Reg had a fantastic day. He threw for a ton of yardage, completed two scoring passes, and was in total command of his team the entire game. He repeatedly demonstrated great arm strength and the ability to throw the football downfield with accuracy. These observations would take on greater meaning later when Reginald and I would become teammates on Virginia State University's football team. I would continually find myself waiting for the guy I played against that day to show up.

Whenever Reg would start railing on about how well he played in this game, I would remind him that with receivers like Bill Tinkler and Leon Stewart and running backs McKeever Brown and James Prince, even the third-string quarterback could have gotten the job done that day. This never had the desired effect, which was to slow him down before he got on a roll.

The debate over who had the best team or the best year would rage on for many years to follow, largely on the basis of this one game. I always took some solace in knowing that it's hard to build a case for being better than undefeated. To Reginald's credit, the "Bragging Rights Game" always ended up the same way: Dunbar 20, Edmondson 0.

CHAPTER 9:

FROM ONE SEASON TO THE NEXT

"Feigned praise is as useless as a donut hole. While we may not always like it, the most useful thing any of us can hear is the truth."
Lin Hart

As the season progressed, football practice would frequently run late, ending well after dark. Our regular after-practice routine was to shower quickly and make our way to the dining hall. This was a 15- to 20-minute walk, carrying us right through the heart of the campus. When the season first began, this trek was marked by the hot humid days of summer. It had always seemed like the perfect time to talk about how we were both going to be stars on the football team and play a leading role in Virginia State's rise to glory.

On this evening, as our group of football players hustled back to the dining hall, the walk had a completely different feeling. By now, my season was going well, but I couldn't help feeling bad about the way things had gone for Reginald. The season was now winding down, and unlike the weather, Reginald's football fortunes had changed very little. We were now into the chilly fall evenings of November, and his descent was complete. He was practically at the bottom of the depth chart, with no signs that things would get better.

Having played against him, I was certain that something was not right with him. Reginald Lewis had been a strong performer in high school. He was also a prideful guy. This made it difficult for him to openly discuss his frustrations. However, on this evening's walk, he seemed more willing to talk about the questions that had been lingering on my mind since the first day of practice. What had gone wrong? Why had he been unable to find his groove and begin playing, as I knew he could?

Halfway into our walk, we found ourselves trailing the rest of the group. We were so caught up in our own conversation that by the time we reached Foster Hall, we hardly noticed the other students busily crisscrossing the campus. Now, after several months of suffering in silence, he seemed willing to do more than make casual references to shoulder soreness. He said his shoulder had been bothering him, and he felt it had screwed up his throwing mechanics. He was understandably concerned about the effect this season's lackluster performance could have on the coaching staff's evaluation for next year.

I was aware that he had made at least one visit to see the physical therapist, but I suggested that he check in with him again and this time open up. If there were issues concerning his shoulder that he had failed to mention on his last visit, he needed to make certain they were addressed this time. He did return to see the therapist, but I never knew the details of his visit. The only thing I knew for sure was that it had no effect on his performance. I was left thinking he had waited too long. His inability to raise his passing game was a continuing source of consternation for the coaches and a source of much disappointment for Reg. It seemed to me that he had clung to the hope that he would catch lightning in a bottle and all would be well once again. It never happened.

By season's end, it had become easier for Reginald to make an honest assessment of his performance. He was also able to reconcile his feeling towards Dewayne Jeter. None of us knew it at the time, but the following year Dewayne Jeter, Al Banks, Reginald, and I would all be card-carrying members of Kappa Alpha Psi fraternity. Jeter had pledged several years ahead of us and as far as Reginald was concerned, he would have long been forgiven.

As for me, Jeter may have been proven partially right in his assessment of my skills as a running back. Throughout my four years at Virginia State, I had success playing at a number of different positions, but the position of lineman was never one of them. It wasn't until my senior year, with the arrival of our new offensive coordinator, Coach Joe Dolphin, that I finally found my way back to my natural position. I made the All Conference team that year, not as a running back, but as a wide receiver.

In the larger scheme of things, Jeter's demanding style of coaching had delivered some valuable truth and in the process reconfirmed something Reginald and I had known before arriving at Virginia State's campus. It was a lesson we had learned from our respective high school coaches Bill "Sugar" Cain and Julian Dyke. "When competing for a job, individual performance matters, and at the end of the day, it's up to the individual to deliver." I never forgot that message, and Reginald F. Lewis's career of success demonstrated that he understood the lesson far better than most.

The Injury—When, Where, and How?

Reginald's life took a significant turn because of his experiences on the football field. The questions I have always had, regarding his shoulder problem were, "What happened? Where did it happen and how did it occur?" I have discussed this with Dewayne Jeter, Albert Banks and other players who were around at the time, and none of us can recall a specific play or tackle causing injury to Reginald's shoulder. As to whether he had shoulder problems, I have no doubt that he did. As his roommate, I was aware he was having problems with his shoulder. However, I have always believed that his arm problems began long before he arrived at Virginia State. The basis for this belief stems from something I noticed when the two of us first began working out during the summer of 1961, prior to reporting to Virginia State.

During those sessions, I would run pass patterns and Reginald would throw passes downfield. It was not long before I began to notice a significant decline in Reginald's arm strength and accuracy. His ability to throw a football deteriorated dramatically. He rarely threw a tight spiral, and he seemed unable to put any distance on his throws.

Having played against him in high school baseball and football, I was familiar with his abilities. There were times when it looked as if Reginald Lewis could throw a ball through a brick wall. He possessed what ball players referred to as a rifle arm. This was further substantiated during my conversations with two of his former Dunbar High School teammates, Leon Stewart and Clarence "Tiger" Davis. Stewart and Davis both acknowledged the fact that Reg, indeed, possessed a rifle arm.

I can recall my high school football coach, Julian Dyke, giving us the scouting report prior to a game against Dunbar. He said, "Their quarterback, Lewis, is a capable leader who passes well. He has a strong throwing arm and good receivers."

In those days, I thought I knew Reginald pretty well, but his tight-lipped approach regarding his shoulder problems always left me a bit puzzled. During the writing of this book, I spoke with his mother, Mrs. Carolyn Fugett, about this chapter of Reginald's life. She said, "You know, Reginald was an extremely private person. If he were hurt, no one would ever know. He was such a private person. He always held his "hold card" close to his chest."

Her reference to a "hold card," as in playing poker, made sense to me. The fact that Reginald was a private person was not something I was unaware of, but I do believe Reginald had a "hold card" that he was not about to reveal. In this case, it may have been his injury. The idea of keeping this "hold card" beyond the prying eyes of others was something he was especially good at. It was a skill that would show up later, over the course of his life. Reginald Lewis always understood that the most important step in playing in any game was finding a way to get in the game. Once in, he knew he would figure out a way to stay in and possibly win. For him, it was simple: Let me get into Virginia State and I will show them I have so much to offer they are going to be glad they let me in.

When considered in that light, not making the football team was not the failure some might have assumed. It is unlikely he would ever have gotten into Virginia State as damaged goods. The key was to get in. He got in and he stayed in. As it turned out, Virginia State was his gateway to Harvard, a successful law career, and his legendary business successes. "Let me in and I will find a way to stay in" would become a consistent theme throughout the course of Reginald F. Lewis's life.

To Build a Dream You Need Some Bricks and Mortar

My parents were a part of the great African-American post World War II migration northward, from Danville, Virginia. They had settled in Baltimore because it was there that my dad and his older brother Jim Hart found work at the docks and in the shipyard. Neither my dad nor my mother had more than an eighth-grade education, but they read the daily newspaper and never missed a nightly news broadcast.

As far back as I can remember, I had always dreamed of being a TV newscaster. Some of my earliest heroes were the broadcasters on the nightly news programs of the 1950s and 60s. These were men like Walter Cronkite, Edward R. Marrow, John Cameron Swayze, and Douglas Edwards. They were on the television, and they were nightly dinner guests in my home. I was in awe of them as examples of great poise, wisdom, and knowledge. They seemed all-knowing, well-spoken masters of language. However, there was one other quality they all had in common. It always seemed like an impenetrable barrier for me. They were all white men. In the early days of television, you had a better chance of finding a Martian in your soup than finding a black news anchor on television. I continued carrying the dream around in my head, because in a dream, anything was possible and it always seemed so much easier. In my dreams, I could go wherever I wanted to go and become whatever I wanted to become.

There were times when I would find a quiet place and just begin ad-libbing my own newscasts. In my deepest baritone voice, I would simply begin making up the news and spouting it out aloud. Most of it was made-up stuff, but who cared? I could report whatever news I wanted to report. For obvious reasons, I had to keep this character secret. If one of my four brothers had found out, they would have had me declared nuts. A move like that would have benefited them greatly in that it would have opened up more sleeping space in our cramped upstairs bedroom and meant one less seat at the crowded dinner table.

By the time Reginald and I had become roommates at Virginia State, I was getting my broadcast fix from one of the most incredible new inventions of the time, a small handheld transistor radio. This little gadget was a wonder of the 1960s and I was lucky enough to have received one for a Christmas present. It was my constant companion, yielding an unending stream of broadcast material and music. Unfortunately, for Reginald, earphones were not as ubiquitous then as they are today. By now, I was airing my fake broadcasts a few minutes, aloud, every day. I considered it a form of practice. Reginald was a guy who had never had to share his room with anyone else, which meant we had to find ways to come to an agreement. It was all made easier because I had agreed to not complain about him playing his tape recorder whenever he was moved to do so. Besides, he would usually crack up laughing at some of the stuff I was saying. Afterwards, he would take on a more serious tone, asking me, "Why do you do that?" My answer was always the same, "My dream job is being a news broadcaster."

It was 1961, and to some of my friends the notion that a black person could become a network TV news announcer seemed like a far-fetched idea. I was soon going to find out that for Reginald Lewis, no idea was far-fetched.

It wasn't long before I began noticing a look of frustration on Reg's face whenever I brought up the subject of becoming an announcer. I came to understand what that look was all about. Thinking about it today, the look is reminiscent of the character played by Bill Murray in the movie *Groundhog Day*. In the movie, Bill Murray's character found himself awakening every morning only to discover that he is doomed to live the same day repeatedly. I think Reg was beginning to feel the same way.

To him, it was as if I had this idea for constructing a grand career but was reluctant to begin building it. Other than blurting out my nightly open-air broadcast, I was doing very little to actually build this splendid career I was dreaming of. I suspect he was thinking, "When are you going to start laying down some bricks and mortar?" The idea of having a dream and not having a plan or the motivation to start working on it was a complete anathema to him. It was like an abstract concept that held little meaning for him. In his own way, he was quietly formulating a way to put a mirror in front of me, a mirror that would enable me to see that there was more I needed to do if I was to have any chance of realizing my dream.

Talk to This Guy

One evening, after putting in several hours of study, I decided to turn in around 11:00 p.m. Reginald had not yet returned to the dormitory. I had just fallen asleep when the door swung open, the light switch was abruptly turned on, and the room was flooded with light. I woke up immediately. It was well past midnight, and the standard roommate courtesy, under such conditions, was to use your desk lamp. I was startled to see Reggie and this other guy entering the room. His guest was a neatly dressed, professional-looking guy. I shouted out in a loud voice, "Reg, what in the hell are you doing, man? Turn off the light. Can't you guys see I'm trying to get some sleep?" His visitor seemed to understand my reaction, but my comments fell upon deaf ears as far as Reg was concerned. He was determined to make a point. That night, he was going to conduct his own version of the *Tonight Show,* and he was going to play the role of Johnny Carson, the host. His unnamed companion was going to be the guest for the evening, and I was going to be his audience.

Reginald pressed on with his own running commentary. "Hart, I want you to meet somebody." He asked his guest to introduce himself. The guy offered a polite apology for having awakened me at such a late hour. The moment I heard him speak, a thought came over me. I didn't recognize his face, but I knew I had heard his voice before. By now, Reggie was fully engaged in his role of the late-night talk-show host. He said, "Hart, this guy is doing exactly what you want to be doing some day. He's in the radio and Television business.

You need to get up and talk to him, right now." Reg pulled up a chair for his guest and sat him right in the middle of the room. By now, his guest was brandishing a half-smile that revealed a slight hint of embarrassment. Finally, the guy introduced himself, saying, "I'm Max Robinson, the evening disk jockey at station WSSV." Well, he just about knocked me out of bed with that bit of news.

In those days Max was a struggling young DJ, spinning records at a local radio station in Petersburg, Virginia. Reggie was aware that I listened to Max regularly. They had bumped into each other that night in Petersburg, and Reginald simply could not pass up this opportunity. He saw this as a way to provide me with the impetus to start laying down some bricks and mortar in building my dream of becoming an announcer. He had convinced Max to come to our dormitory to share his experiences with me.

The three of us spent the rest of the night discussing the future prospects of African-Americans in the radio and television business. Max and Reg were both supportive of my desire to enter the field of broadcasting. Afterwards, I could see Reginald felt good about having pulled off this late-night venture successfully. There was nothing he loved more than surprising people this way. I made it a little easier for him to take a bow on this one. I really appreciated what he had done and told him so. By reaching out to introduce me to Max, he had accomplished something much bigger than the introduction. By his actions, he was saying, "Hart, I believe you actually have the ability and the voice to become a radio broadcaster." It was a vote of confidence coming from him.

That was the most important thing that happened that night. It lent credibility to the idea of using my voice and speaking ability as essential parts of my career planning. Max was a person already doing it. He was an African-American broadcaster working at a white station, and in the south, no less. He was living proof that it was possible.

For Reginald Lewis, it was pretty simple: If you're going to build something, you have to be willing to do something. I needed to start applying some bricks and mortar in building my own dream. From that night on, I never wavered in my understanding of the power of speech and voice when it came to opening doors and influencing people.

I never worked in the radio and television broadcast industry, but many years later I enrolled and completed the St. Louis–based Broadcast Center's course in broadcast development. By that time, my career in the telecommunications industry was well under way. I saw the Broadcast Center experience as another way of continuing to strengthen my presentation and communication skills. It was these skills that I would come to rely upon in advancing my career over the course of my many years as a business executive, professional speaker, and leadership coach. That late-night meeting in 1961 was a big deal for me. Thanks to Reginald and Max Robinson, I found my bricks and mortar.

If you're unfamiliar with the name Max Robinson, you might be interested to know that Max went on to play a key role in the evolution of broadcast television in the United States. In 1978, he made history when ABC TV executive Roone Arledge hired him to be a co-anchor of the network's evening news broadcast. When he gave him the job, Mr. Arledge bestowed upon Max a very significant title. Max Robinson became the first black man to anchor a nightly network news broadcast in the history of American broadcasting. Max was working at ABC's Chicago affiliate at the time. He was teamed with Frank Reynolds in Washington and Peter Jennings in London. From 1978 to 1984, they co-anchored ABC's evening news. Max's assignment was a major breakthrough in helping to bring down years of racial discrimination in the broadcast industry. I think of him as the person who eventually removed that Martian from my alphabet soup. Max died December 20, 1988.

Privacy Is a Priority—The Vanilla Wafer Caper

It is written that possession is nine-tenths of the law. My rough translation of this adage is, "He that has, not only gets to keep, but also gets to dole out."

Given my financial status, I was a guy who was always squirreling stuff away in an effort to make it last longer. I had picked up the habit as a means of keeping my stash away from the clutches of my brothers, Rod and Tony. It would be fair to say that I was not above poaching their stashes too.

I recall as a youngster of 12 getting my first real job working as a stock boy at the corner store. The store was called Leon's. Whenever I received my meager pay of three dollars, I would save half and spend the rest on something I liked. My favorite thing to buy was a box of cookies and a big orange

Nehi soda. Buying it in his store always seemed to delight Leon. I was too young to realize it at the time, but spending a significant portion of my pay in his store was pretty close to Leon having me work there free.

The habit of stashing things away followed me when I went off to college. I soon realized that with Reginald, as my roommate there was no need to be so insecure about such things. He was not the kind of guy who would ever invade your stuff or your privacy. We both had respect for each other's privacy and territory.

One evening, I was retrieving a box of vanilla wafers from the top of my closet. I had them encased in a plastic bag, which helped keep them fresh. Noticing this, Reg asked, "Man I could use something to snack on right now. How about letting me have a few of those vanilla wafers?" I said, "Sure." I was certain this was not the first time he had had a vanilla wafer, but he reacted as if he was discovering them for the first time. This set up a regular arrangement, during which one of us would purchase a box of vanilla wafers and, in the evening, we would sit in our room sharing with the other guy. It was the perfect setting to discuss football, girls, or class work.

Whenever this was going on, it became our shared task to maintain a proper level of security in the room. There was only one other guy who had an open pass to our room: Al Banks. Al was like the third cog in the wheel. It seemed like he spent as much time in our room as we did. For all others it was "Keep Out."

We both knew there were guys on the football team who made a practice of popping in at night, unannounced, to see if you had anything to eat. If these same guys ever discovered that we were hoarding a stash of goodies, we were going to get way more attention than we wanted. They would have descended upon our room like a horde of locusts pressuring us to share the goodies. It would have been a surge of biblical proportions. Knowing this we always adhered to a strict rule. Whenever we had our stash in full view, we kept the door locked. Surprise walk-in visits were not allowed. Given both our tendencies to guard our privacy, this practice fit nicely into our worldview. We always kept a keen eye out for the guys who tended to prowl the hallways late at night, looking for something to eat.

As you might guess, our passion for security sometimes led to awkward moments. There was one moment in particular that left us with a story that we would tell frequently over the years that followed. On the surface, it seemed rather trivial but it gets to the heart of how Reginald viewed his possessions and his privacy.

Reg and I were up late one night having a loud debate about something, and Reg let his guard down. The rule was, "He who has his snacks out is the one who makes sure the door is locked." On this night, he forgot to lock the door before drawing down his stash of vanilla wafers. One of our teammates, a hulking lineman, happened to pass by our room. Because of his build, I had affectionately given him the nickname "Juggernaut Jones," a cartoon character who had frequently appeared in the old National Bohemian Beer commercials that ran on TV in Baltimore. Overhearing all the noise, Jug just opened the door and sauntered right in.

We looked up and he was just standing there. "Oh! Oh!" We both whispered. We knew what was coming next. Jug said he was just stopping by to visit. It didn't take long before he spotted Reg's unattended box of Nabisco vanilla wafers sitting opened on the desk. Upon spying those cookies, Juggernaut's eyes went into "Hyper Glaze." He said to Reginald, "You mind if I have some of those?" Reg acted as though he had not heard Jug. Juggernaut persisted and said, "Hey, how about letting me have some of those cookies?" Reg was okay with sharing, but you could see he had a real reluctance about turning Jugs loose on his precious snack.

Juggernaut was a big man, weighing close to 250 lbs. Reg was just a tad over 5' 9" and weighed just over 175 lbs. Reginald reluctantly gave in, but I could see he was determined to maintain firm control over the distribution process. His hands had formed a vice-like grip on the box. It was the kind of grip that said, "One or two wafers and no more." Of course, I could see in Juggernaut's eyes that he had designs on a much bigger haul than that. He was clearly not going to settle for just one or two cookies. With a big smile on his face, Jug was totally committed to getting as many wafers as he could. His beefy right hand went deep into the box and began to corral as many vanilla wafers as he could wrap his paw around. As he drug his hand up the side of the box, cookies started to fall onto the floor. Reginald was not to be deterred. This was a life-or-death struggle over those vanilla wafers, and because of Juggernaut's sheer size and strength, I knew Reginald was not going to win. I thought to myself, "Oh shit, this is about to get ugly."

To appreciate what was going on at that moment, you had to know that Juggernaut was not a bully. We had only known him for a short while, and neither of us had ever seen him angry. He was usually a good-natured guy, but now he had been overcome by his late-night hunger spasm, and he was not about to yield to proper decorum. Sharing protocol be damned, it was full steam ahead. This whole incident took only a couple of minutes, but it seemed like an eternity. After securing his bounty and seemingly pleased with his good fortune, Jugs politely said "Good night," turned around and left the room.

At first, Reginald did not take too kindly to the idea that I thought it was funny, but after a while, he was able to see the humor as I had. Jugs had left without ever realizing that he had provided us with a story that, over the years, we could always count on to bring us both to laughter and tears.

While we were roommates, we never let it happen again. Reg made certain that the door to our room was always locked whenever the good stuff was out. Whenever he left something out, it was with his awareness. If it was going to be shared, it was going to be shared on his terms.

Many years after his passing I was sharing this story with Reginald's driver, Lucien Stoutt. Lucien said, "Mr. Lewis always did enjoy a good cookie."

CHAPTER 10:
THE HILLMAN—TRIBUTE AND TRIUMPH

---

*"Overcome your greatest fears by taking them on in a way
that gives you a reasonable chance of survival."*
Lin Hart

When you are 17 years old, broke, and trying to find your way in the world, a lot of funny stuff happens along the way. At the same time, you learn a lot about yourself and your friends too.

Christmas break was ending, and I had started to make plans for my return trip from Baltimore back to Virginia State's campus. I was ready to shell out the bucks for a one-way bus ticket when Reginald Lewis called and said he was taking his car back to campus. He wanted to know if I would like to ride back with him. I paused for a moment and then answered, "Yes." Now we would both be returning to campus in his car, the Hillman.

The Hillman was a British-made automobile, and it was Reginald's pride and joy. We had tooled around the city the past summer in the Hillman, so I was familiar with the car's rather finicky ways. From my experience, The Hillman's electrical system was a bit unpredictable. It relied upon a variety of fuses, and whenever one of those fuses blew out, everything would come to a dead stop. Keeping the Hillman on the road seemed to depend upon Reginald having invested in an ample supply of replacement fuses. I understood both the risk and the economics of my decision. Back then, when gas was insanely cheap, pitching in to help pay for the Hillman's gas was a lot better deal than having to spring for a Trailway's bus ticket.

While the state of my finances weighed heavily upon my decision, there were other considerations influencing me as well. First, Reg had offered me the opportunity to ride with him. He could have picked someone else, but he had asked me. I knew he was not keen on letting just anybody ride in his car. You never saw him with a car crammed full of dudes on a joy ride. The fact that he had frequently reached out to me in the summer when he was driving around Baltimore in his prized Hillman said a lot to me. Finally, I did not want to see my friend get stuck on the highway alone if the Hillman failed him.

For some reason, we had gotten a late start. A morning departure would have assured us the benefit of more daylight in which to travel. Instead, we left around late afternoon. The sun was still bright, and a cloudless sky reassured us that our travels would be trouble free. At least that was what I thought when Reginald pulled up in front of my house and honked his horn. We doubled back to his house, which was a few blocks away on Mosher Street. I remember his mom giving him a brief lecture about being safe, and we were on our way.

In those days, Petersburg, Virginia, was about a 3-hour ride from Baltimore. I figured we had plenty of daylight in which to make the trip. We had barely gotten under way, however, when we got our first sign that this was not going to be an uneventful trip. As we made our way onto Franklin Street, headed east, we had to make a stop. Reg was concerned with a balky stem on one of his tires, so to be on the safe side we decided to stop and put some air in the tire. To give you some perspective, we were about a couple of miles from our starting point when this tire problem came up. This was not a good sign. The good news was it was not the electrical system and the bad news was that we now had to hope that the balky tire would hold up.

After taking care of the tire, we continued east, on Franklin Street. This was a bit of a surprise to me. I wondered why we weren't making our way in a southerly direction as one would expect if we were heading to Virginia. At that point, Reginald slipped in the first of his surprise announcements. He said, "Oh, I forgot to tell you, I have to make a stop before we leave town." My first thought was, "Uh Oh! Here we go. Who knows when we're going to get out of town?" I decided to keep my feelings under wraps. After all, the guy was gracious enough to offer me a ride back to campus. The least I could do was to accept some incidental inconvenience.

It turned out that our first stop was his father's business. It was a small, but neat, restaurant located in East Baltimore. This was the first time I had been to the place. I was impressed to know that his dad actually owned this small business. I took a seat at the counter, while Reg and his father were engaged in a conversation. I had no idea what it was about, but it seemed like it was important. They convened to the rear of the restaurant, so I resigned myself to being there for a while. I took a seat at the counter, thinking how cool it must be to own your own business.

The time seemed to drag by slowly. I recall looking at my watch and thinking we had better get going before we let too much daylight pass. This was 1961. The last thing I wanted to have happen was for the two of us to be stuck on some dark highway in the middle of the night in Virginia. I saw this as a real cause for concern.

Once Reginald finished his conversation with his father, we were under way again, or so I thought. As we were pulling away from the restaurant, he offered up a second surprise announcement. He said, "Oh, Hart, I forgot to mention it, but I have to stop by the downtown library to drop off a couple of books I borrowed." We would now have to drive to the downtown branch of Baltimore's Enoch Pratt public library, a short distance away.

While I was mildly disappointed at having to make another detour, this one held some interest for me. My library visits had always been limited to the Walbrook branch, which was within walking distance from my house. As a kid growing up in Baltimore in the 1950s, I had walked past the downtown central branch building many times on shopping trips with my mother, but I had never gone in. It was an impressive facility, because of its size, location, and architecture. I was starting to feel less peeved by this second detour. I was actually looking forward to getting a chance to see what it looked like inside this big library.

Once Reg dropped off the books, I turned to him and said, "Hey man, we gotta get rolling." We made a final stop to fill up the gas tank, after which Reginald deftly steered the Hillman onto the highway. We were finally headed south and on our way back to Virginia State's campus in Petersburg. Looking up at the sky, I finally had to accept that there was no way we were going to make it back before nightfall.

As we were making our way past the Washington D.C area, I was feeling like I needed to give the Hillman a big vote of confidence. The car was purring like a kitten, and we were making good time. That didn't last very long. Soon we began hearing rather worrying noises. It sounded like the car was starting to have power problems. It was beginning to look like I would have to rescind my vote of confidence for the Hillman. Reginald put on his most reassuring used-car salesman's face in an attempt to reassure me that whatever it was, it wasn't serious. The car chugged along. As we were passing nearby Fredericksburg, Virginia, the Hillman came to a complete stop.

Reginald was prepared this time. He reached into the glove compartment, grabbed a fuse, slammed it into the fuse box, and we were off and running again. I was thinking that I hadn't seen many fuses in that glove compartment and as far as I knew you couldn't pick up fuses for the Hillman at just any old place. It seemed to me that this fuse problem was going to add a little more anxiety to our trip. Still, I heaved a sigh of relief, thinking, "Hey, not bad. My man Reg is on the case."

I would soon discover that "My man Reg" would end up being on the case a lot that evening, popping in those fuses.

Soon it was nightfall, and we still had a lot of road to cover. The situation was not looking good. The car had once again come to a halt. We were now down to our last fuse. We both agreed that we should try to push the car to get it started this time. If we could do it, we would be able to preserve that last fuse as our bailout, in case we needed it further down the road. Pushing it had worked before, but the problem with that solution was that I became the designated pusher. There was no way Reginald was going to let anybody else behind the wheel of his car.

Actually, we both pushed until we got the Hillman going at a good rate of speed, then Reggie would jump in the car and begin to steer. My job was to push and push for as long as it took to get that engine to turn over. This time, it worked.

We were under way again, but we were both riding on a hope and a prayer.

We hadn't gone very far when it happened again. Now we had a decision to make. This seemed like a good time to discuss our options. We knew from the road signs there was a small community just ahead. We could use the last fuse to get us there, and we could catch a bus back to campus. I didn't know Reginald's situation, but with just enough money in my pocket for bus fare, this strategy made sense to me. I had simply lost confidence in the Hillman's ability to get us back to campus. The look on Reginald's face conveyed a different story.

In considering a new strategy, there were three important factors to be acknowledged. First, this was 1961. Next, we were two black guys. Finally, in the next 30 to 40 miles past that town up ahead, there was nothing but a pitch-black, Virginia highway. If we put that last fuse in and it blew out in the middle of nowhere, the resulting scenario could spell big trouble for the both of us. Throw in the fact that the temperature was beginning to drop and our situation was becoming even dicier. That fuse would have to hold up until we got to the other side of that 40 mile dark zone or, better yet, all the way back to campus.

Sensing a decline in my level of enthusiasm for the mission, Reginald Lewis suddenly turned into Frederick Douglass. He launched off into a speech about why we should put the fuse in and make a mad dash, right through the darkest, most desolate part of our trip. He began by saying, "Hart, I see this as a test of wills. It's like we have a challenge. Can the two of us get this car back to campus?" He went on, "I think the last thing we should do is quit."

I wasn't some country hayseed. I knew exactly what was going on in Reg's mind. There was no way he was going to leave his prized possession by the side of the road or all alone in some small town where who knows what would happen to it.

He continued on. "I'm taking this as a personal challenge to finish what we started. How sweet it's gonna be if, after dealing with all this crap, we actually get this car back to campus." Having heard enough, I turned to him and said, "Reggie, spare me the speech. You know I'm not going to leave you out here alone. Get in the freakin' car and let's see if we can get this thing going again." We popped in that last fuse, and we were off and running.

Luck must have been with us, because we made it through the unlit patch of road. It had been the most fitful 30–40 miles I had ever traveled. There were no cell phones in those days, and emergency phones were few and far between. Not only had it been pitch black, the cold had settled in. About 20 miles from Colonial Heights, Virginia, the Hillman stopped dead in its tracks again. We could see the lights and an overpass up ahead. I said, "That's it, I'm out of here. Let's go, Reg. We can find some place to catch a bus from here and come back for the car later."

Reg acted as though he didn't hear me and began pushing the car, while at the same time saying "We're almost there." I looked at him and thought, "Can you believe this shit? This guy is crazy." Then it struck me. "Okay. Given where we are, it might take only a couple more push-starts and we could make it to Colonial Heights." If we could make it to Colonial Heights, we would be within walking distance of the campus.

By now, Reginald was in a heightened state of emotion, raging on about how far we had come and how this thing was a test of wills. I stood there with my eyes fixed on the ground, thinking Reginald Lewis had made this entire episode personal. It had become a contest, with the two of us going against this stubborn car. After a moment's reflection, I looked up and there was Reg leaning on the driver side door in an effort to push-start this stalled car down the graveled shoulder on the highway. Upon seeing him locked in this Titanic struggle to get the car going, I finally yielded and began running to catch up to him. At the same time, I began shouting, "Get your crazy butt in the car. If you're this damned determined to get this car back to campus, then I'm crazy enough to hang in here with you."

We got it started once again, but when I jumped into the car this time I had a different feeling. I had a much more determined disposition. My attitude was a bit cockier. I even had a smirk on my face. I began thinking we could actually do this. It now seemed as if victory was within sight. Reg's enthusiasm and downright stubbornness had rubbed off on me. This was no longer just a challenge. It had become a cause. It had become our Mount Everest. It was our fourth-quarter drive in the waning moments of the championship game. This task had to be completed. As I was sitting in the front seat with my arms crossed, I remember thinking how sweet it was going to be when we get the Hillman back to campus.

As good as that moment felt, it was not quite a done deal yet. We managed to make it to within a short distance from the campus before finally conking out again. We came to a stop across from the football stadium, at the corner of 4th Avenue and East River Road. We both paused for a moment to catch our breath, and then it happened. We both broke out into the most incredible laughter you could imagine. There we stood, with the Hillman, perched atop this medium downgrade. All that remained to complete our long, frustrating journey would be to give the Hillman a slight push to get it started downhill. With just a slight push, we could both claim our conquest and triumphantly coast the rest of the way, down the hill and onto the campus parking lot.

What a moment! It was incredible. It was exhilarating, and it was success. We both ran alongside the Hillman, laughing all the way. Finally came the last push, and with that push it was over. We both jumped into the front seat of the car. We sat there as the Hillman gradually picked up speed on its way down the hill. The smiles on our faces stretched from ear to ear. We had actually pulled it off. We had done what I had thought was impossible. To my surprise, it was sweet. It was very sweet. It was real sweet."

When this episode in our lives happened, it was a big deal for a while, but the full impact of what had happened wouldn't register on me until many years later. Before this incident with the Hillman, I had little awareness of what it was like to push myself beyond reasonable limits to accomplish a big task. Now, because of Reginald's persistence, I was beginning to appreciate how the principles of motivation, influence, and will power could be applied to other endeavors outside of sports.

Reginald Lewis was well known for having a big ego and for being prone to speaking in outsized terms. There were times when I had felt he was simply ego-tripping, but Reginald had discovered something, and now I was picking up on it. He understood that, before you can talk someone else into helping you to achieve something extraordinary, you had to talk yourself into believing you were capable of pulling it off.

Another important lesson stemming from the events of that night on the roadside in Virginia, was Reginald understood that he couldn't get me fully committed behind his vision of success by focusing solely on his own self-interest. From the moment our troubles began, he knew it would not be enough to simply say, "Hart, help me get my car back to campus." To get me fully engaged on that cold night would require something bigger, something much more compelling.

Reginald knew I didn't want to leave him, but to get me past my own doubts he had to appeal to my self-interest as well as his own. He elected to do it with a sports metaphor. He understood that by framing the task as a contest, as a challenge to be overcome, he could stimulate my competitive juices. In doing so, he stood a much better chance of getting me committed for the long haul. Knowing me as he did, he could just about predict how I would feel once we got the Hillman to the top of the last hill. Framing that final picture as a contest with the two of us ending up standing on the hill together and saying how sweet it is, was the right ticket to get me in the game.

CHAPTER 11:

A FALLEN STAR AND THE AFTERMATH OF INJURY

"Defeat is a grand teacher. Work like hell to figure out how to apply your new learning in ways that work for you and not against you."
Lin Hart

Several months had passed since the end of football season. During the months that followed, Reginald may have made a couple of visits to the therapist, but I have no recollection of a major rehab program involving his arm. This may have merely been a reflection of the time. Intensive off-season rehab, in those days, was usually reserved for athletes who suffered major injuries, such as a broken bones or serious fractures. Athletes were usually left on their own to work off any kinks or aches to their extremities. The philosophy was, "Time heals all wounds."

With spring football rapidly approaching, those players who had not performed well during the past season were now on the bubble. Coaches were fond of reminding players that unless they met expectations they could lose their scholarships. In those days, a guaranteed four-year football scholarship was unheard of on our campus. A scholarship was performance-based and renegotiable every year. Aside from keeping your grades up, a player's best chance of insuring his scholarship was to have had a great season, a great spring, and to have remained healthy. If you came up short in any of these three areas, you would be in serious jeopardy of losing your scholarship.

Reginald had every reason to be concerned, yet he never showed signs that he was. Maybe it was a bit naive on my part, but I never thought there was any chance he would lose his scholarship. While he would still have an occasional harsh word for the coaches, it contained very little of the bitterness he had exhibited over most of the last season. However, he demonstrated a continued willingness to accept that he had not performed at his best over that period.

In the few times leading up to spring practice that I had watched him throwing the football, his mechanics appeared to have been off a bit. He still seemed unable to throw the tight spiral I had seen him throw back at Dunbar High School. Nevertheless, Reg seemed confident that he could return to his old high school form. Of the returning quarterbacks, the top candidates would all be sophomores, just like him. There was no clear-cut heir apparent. The road ahead was pretty clear. There would be plenty of room for him at the top of the depth chart, but only if he could somehow show the coaches something during spring practice.

As spring football arrived, I remained hopeful, but it was more of the same. By now, his throwing motion seemed to have been altered, and his mechanics were still failing him. Reginald still looked the part of a top-flight quarterback, that is, until he was required to throw the football. Things were not going well. The longer it went on, the more he struggled.

After spring football practice ended, I recall him returning to the room one afternoon with a downcast, somber look on his face. He told me that he had just been informed by Coach Lawson that he would not be awarded a scholarship for the coming season. Reginald was disappointed and angry. I mean he was really angry. I had never known him to use profanity to the extent that he did that afternoon. I recall probing him for clarification. I thought maybe he had left something out. Maybe the coach had simply reduced his scholarship money but not actually withdrawn the entire scholarship. Reg said, "No. That S.O.B. was very clear. I'm not going to be offered any money for next year." As he sat on the side of his bed, he made a valiant effort to fend off his anger and his disappointment. I continued trying to find words of consolation and encouragement. I was not very successful.

A short while later, I could see he had collected himself. He seemed resolute yet resigned to accepting the inevitability of his situation. I thought this would be a good time to bring up the subject of law school. I said, "This was a lousy break, but all is not lost." I started to suggest that he could try to walk on next season, without a scholarship, but that thought seemed too improbable. The chemistry between Reg and Coach Lawson seemed to have been tainted well beyond repair. I started thinking, what would I have done if this had happened to me. I really had no idea what this meant for Reg either. I knew he had come from a working-class family, and I knew they would be solidly behind him. Beyond that thought, I had little insight into how he was going to remain at Virginia State.

I brought up the subject of law school. Reginald always seemed energized whenever he spoke about the likelihood of law school. In spite of the rather somber mood in the room, it was clear that he had not taken his sights off that goal. He was quick to acknowledge that not all was lost. Despite his anger at Coach Lawson's decision, Reginald seemed ready to acknowledge that the time had finally come for him to put aside the notion of becoming a major football star. Instead, he seemed to have been saying, "Now I've got to move on to Plan B."

I never knew if anything I said that day had any impact upon Reginald at all. It was times like this when it was impossible to know what Reginald was thinking. I never knew him to play cards, but he always could deliver a great poker face. The message I struggled to send that day was that I felt really bad about what had happened to him, but I never thought it was going to keep him from doing what he had set out to do. The one thing I knew for sure was that while it might have been the end of the scholarship, it was definitely not the end of Reginald F. Lewis.

When it was all over, Reg left the room, heading off to some place unknown to me. I found myself staring out the lone window in the room. I was wondering what would happen if Reginald did not return for the next semester. What would it feel like if he were not around? In those days, members of the football team usually roomed with teammates. Losing his scholarship would bring that stage of our friendship to an end. It would also change the dynamics of the friendship that existed between Reginald, Al, and me. We had always been a threesome. We would still be friends, but because of the overwhelming amount of time Al and I would have to dedicate to football, it would mean less hanging out together as the "Baltimore Guys."

In the spring of 1962, a significant chapter of young Reginald F. Lewis's life was closed shut for good. He had accepted it for what it was: another one of life's lessons on the road to the rest of his life. What I had no way of knowing was that another door was opening at the same moment. It was a door that Reginald was destined to blow off its hinges on his way to becoming a significant, historical figure.

CHAPTER 12:

PRINCIPLES, HABITS, AND BELIEFS

"Those who say it can't be done are usually interrupted by others doing it."
James Baldwin

Reginald was clearly the most purpose-driven person I ever met, but unless you spent a lot of time with him, you probably would have been unaware of just how driven he was. He operated as though he was absolutely certain of his purpose for being here on earth. His purpose was to achieve something on a grand scale. Getting it done would involve hard work, but that was never going to be a deterrent for him, not as long as he could see how the work fit in with his goal-driven purpose.

His approach to doing things was often different from other students. Reg was not someone who spent a lot of time worrying about what others thought of him. As long as it was consistent with his beliefs about success, that was what he was going to do. Success for Reginald was never going to be as simple as just being good at something. For success to have real meaning, it would have to astound the average person. It would have to have scale and significant impact. Reginald's mental model for success required achieving success on a grand scale.

Today, experts tell us that our mental models are representative of how we see the world and all the things that surround us. That was certainly true of Reginald. His mental model formed his inside pictures of the outside world. These pictures were a major influence in determining how he would ultimately navigate his way through and around the obstacles he faced later in his life.

A frequently discussed topic with Reginald was the way in which people viewed opportunity and how they chose to look for opportunities. Reg believed there was an optimal way of looking at opportunities and finding ways to take advantage of them. He believed that standing in the way of most people was the traditional view that our opportunities lie somewhere in the future. They were always just around the corner and could only be accessed through the passage of time. It was a common expression for people to say, "When I get enough time or when I get sufficient money, I'll be able to do this or do that." In his view, it was limiting to think solely in future terms when it came to the acquisition of opportunities. He operated from the perspective that the pursuit of success required the ability to see the opportunities in real time. It was always his contention that the best opportunities existed in real time, in the moment.

When viewed this way, we were always in a constant state of opportunity, surrounded by new possibilities every day and every minute. The fact that most people operated without a plan or a specific set of goals meant they lacked the vision to see the vast number of opportunities being presented to them every day. This was a key construct in Reginald's mental model.

He hadn't come by this mental model by accident. From the very beginning, he always had the benefit of great role models. He was blessed with lots of extended family who provided him with a sturdy and positive support system. The one person I'm most familiar with is his mother, Mrs. Carolyn Fugett. It was she, sounding the regular drum beat of inspirational messages, who instilled in him the notion that great accomplishments were possible for a black man, even if the hurdles seemed insurmountable in the 1960s. She made certain that he understood that, even with the support of family, it would be up to him to begin forging his own way to success. He would have to craft a model for success that would withstand the headwinds of discrimination and prejudice. In the end, he would craft a model for success that was much bigger than anything any of us, his peers, could have imagined.

Millionaire Mindset

Reginald F. Lewis could be pleasant and articulate but fully capable of becoming angry and argumentative at the drop of a pin. He thought highly of himself, and there were times when he would travel well beyond conventional thinking to make his point. Sometimes when he was pressing his case, it became difficult to distinguish between candor, bluster, and BS. We would often find ourselves in this predicament whenever Reg was trying to make the case for expanding someone else's view of what was possible. The story that follows is an illustration of what I mean.

Reginald, Al, and I would frequently convene to our dormitory room, 122 Williams Hall, to engage in debate over any number of issues. These closed-door sessions allowed for a lot of serious discussion, but you could also count on there being a lot of laughs. On this particular evening, the topic was money. Money was always a favorite topic of discussion with us because none of us had any. The question at that time was, "What was the most money you could see yourself making in a year?" It's important to keep in mind the effect of inflation since the early 60s.

I was first up, and I quickly blurted out a figure of $6,000. Yes, that's right. I would have been satisfied with a $6,000 annual salary. Al chimed in, "Hart, you're not thinking big enough. I want some big money. I have to have at least $12,000 a year." Reggie, as was his habit, wanted to go last. This provided him with the ideal opportunity to upstage everyone else in the conversation. Sitting at his desk with a smirk on his face, he chimed in, "You guys just don't get it." At this point, he threw out a number that was much greater than anything either Al or I had been thinking.

Upon hearing him, Al and I looked at each other, and we both started laughing. I said, "Man, are you crazy? Black folks aren't making that kind of money." I remember laughing because it seemed like such an overreach that I found it hard to take him seriously.

It also occurred to me that Reggie was just being Reg. It was not uncommon for him to try to upstage everyone else in a discussion this way. He always seemed to take special delight in trying to demonstrate that he had a better grasp of the situation than anyone else did.

In a subsequent conversation between the two of us, Reg proclaimed, that it was his intention to become a millionaire. I recall, once again, finding humor in his remarks, but Reginald was steadfast. I said, "Reggie, are you really serious about this millionaire stuff?" He sat up on the edge of his bed and said, "Hell, yes I am." I said, "Reg, you are one cocky guy." He then flashed his trademark, gapped-tooth smile, turned off the lights, and drifted off to sleep.

It was in moments like this, when friends and classmates simply assumed Reg was trying to upstage the group. In fact what he was saying was, "I'm never going to be satisfied with just being successful in a small way." At the time he made reference to wanting to become a millionaire, the term carried a lot more weight than it does today. It was certainly larger than anything I was able to comprehend, yet it was instructive. It represented a major component of Reg's mental model for success. Successful execution against his model required that it be something big and it was going to be measured in dollars, lots of dollars.

There was also another piece of his model for success that did not go unnoticed by me. His success would be made even sweeter if it merited great significance in the eyes of other similarly successful people.

CHAPTER 13:

GOTTA KEEP GOING

"So, boy, don't you turn back."
Langston Hughes

It was now the beginning of Reginald's sophomore year and he was more determined than ever in moving forward. He would adhere to his mother's advice: "Reginald! Now you gotta go full academic."

He had steeled himself for the task ahead. He had spent the summer on campus, working and attending summer school classes. The fact that he was no longer on the football team meant we were no longer roommates. Earlier that summer, Reg had told me he was not interested in finding a new roommate. Instead, he was going to settle for one of the few single rooms on the first floor in Langston Hall. I held out little hope that he could pull this off, but he did. Al Banks and I were now roommates and living in Langston Hall. This would put him just a few doors away from Al and me. It didn't seem to matter that much. Regardless of where he was, we felt that the three of us were still going to remain a very close-knit group.

Reflecting on Planning

With his books tucked firmly under one arm and his trench coat collar pulled high to shield him from the wind, the former football player, Reginald Lewis, could be seen making his way across campus. Reginald always walked with an unusually long stride, belying his 5' 9" stature. It made him look bigger and more purposeful. His deep-set eyes and furrowed brow gave him a look of determination that left little doubt that he was a young man on a serious mission.

His course would now have to be different. It would not require a complete makeover, but it was going to require a serious revision to his plan. There was some good news in all of this for Reginald. If it required planning, he was going to be playing to his strength

In 1973, I recall standing in a conference room by myself, staring at a gigantic flow chart posted on the wall. For a fleeting moment, I found myself having a momentary flashback to my days in college. I was thinking about how Reginald had always been so meticulous in laying out, in writing, his plans for the week, the month, and the year. Often, it would appear to be nothing more than a bunch of cryptic notes that only he could understand. The whole routine had always seemed like overkill to me. This would invariably lead to a discussion between the two of us about how planning played into the lives of certain people who were successful. After a while, it began to make sense. We both concluded that most successful people got that way because they were planners. They never left anything to chance. This was the thought that dominated my mind as I stood staring at that flow chart on the wall.

At that moment, the flow chart on the wall represented the single biggest challenge of my young career. I was working in AT&T's manufacturing division, Western Electric. This was the first major project following my promotion. My new job was to lead the group responsible for the introduction of new and changed products at the company's Baltimore Works. The place had a population of over 2,000 people. My new assignment had catapulted me right into the middle of every key operation in the place. The chart on the wall was a mock-up of the process we would use to introduce an important series of products into the manufacturing process at the location's apparatus shop. It involved a myriad of simultaneous but seemingly unrelated activities. Anything as much as a hiccup in any one those activities would seriously jeopardize the manufacturing process of products and systems throughout the place.

As I stared at the chart, the refrain that kept playing repeatedly in my head was, "nothing should ever be left to chance or random circumstance." It was like a repeating verse that kept careening from one side of my brain to the other. Nothing must ever be left to chance or random circumstance. Nothing must ever be left to random chance or circumstance.

Strict adherence to that single planning thought would eventually deliver a series of successes during my time on that assignment and throughout the rest of my life.

Getting Under Way

Reginald would have to engineer his rebound from the first major setback of his young life. If he was going to have any chance of making it through Virginia State over the next three years and achieving his dream of becoming a lawyer, he would have to come up with a new game plan.

Always accustomed to being the "Big Man on Campus," he was now just one of many students on campus. Getting acclimated to his new role would require that he refocus his attention on excelling in a different way. Excellence still mattered, but campus celebrity would have to matter a lot less. For the first time in his life, he would have to carry the profile of "student" rather than "student/athlete." Letting go was not going to be easy, but he seemed resigned to it. There was little he could do to reclaim his old status anyway.

I could not help thinking what a tough blow this must have been for him. I had expected that he would become surly and dismissive when it came to the football team, but to my surprise, he was just the opposite. Instead a becoming a resentful, brooding critic, he became more openly supportive in his comments with respect to the players and the team. This was especially true in our relationship. He paid particular attention to my play on the field and would often offer both praise and constructive critiques following games. Reginald had been a student of the game of football for years. I often found his suggestions helpful. He had responded in a way that I had not expected.

He also seemed to be more at ease with himself. He began to show brief flashes of humility, which allowed our friendship to require less maintenance. Reginald Lewis was always going to be someone with strong opinions, but for a brief period in 1962, he seemed less interested in beating you up with them.

Always the competitor, Reginald was now confronted with a new challenge. To start, he had to acknowledge that the game had now changed for him. His competitive instincts would now have to be directed toward a new kind of playing field and a different kind of contest. The psychological and emotional boost that came with being a football star and big man on campus would have to be re-channeled in a different way.

He could see that with everything that had taken place, all but one of his original goals still remained intact. However, achieving them had not been made any easier by the events of his recent past. They were still substantial, and they would require a full-frontal assault if he was to succeed. The key would lie in making sure he brought to this new game the same passion and confidence he had always brought to football. New planning would be required to hit his new targets over the next three years:

- Dramatically improve his grades
- Earn enough money to help pay his bills
- Pledge Kappa Alpha Psi fraternity
- Graduate in four years
- Gain admittance into a prestigious law school

Bringing it all to a successful conclusion would require nailing all five tasks. Yes, he had suffered a setback, but this setback was now going to serve as his launch pad. It would be from this point that he would begin the process of recasting himself as a winner. He would introduce a bit of strategic thinking, continue deploying his well-developed planning skills, and begin the serious business of becoming an entrepreneur with a goal of earning additional money to replace his lost scholarship.

In considering a new strategy, his choice of close friends would become critical. Working would consume a large chunk of his free time and he realized he could ill afford to spend a lot of idle time simply hanging out. Reginald was not the kind of person who required a lot of attention. He never felt as though he needed to be friends with everybody. As his high school teammate Leon Stewart had pointed out, Reginald was not "anti-social." However, in his new role as student non-athlete, it was of paramount importance that he remain socially relevant. Reginald never wanted to be seen as some average Joe, logging time, moving aimlessly from one end of the campus to the other. He wanted to be among those who could stimulate him intellectually and engage him in an exchange of ideas and opinions. This would ultimately boil down to a few friends with whom he sought to have an ongoing "mind meld." These folks fit neatly into four groups:

- Prominent campus athletes and students
- Highly visible members of fraternities and sororities
- Certain influential faculty members
- All attractive women

For the most part, these were people whose conversation, academic pursuits and personal goals mirrored those of his own. They were well-informed, ambitious, and popular. Reginald saw them as the movers and shakers on campus. This meant there would be some social benefit in maintaining a relationship with them.

While such friendships were important to him, he could be quite casual when it came to maintaining them. It always appeared to me that Reginald was inviting this group of people into his world on his terms. One thing you could be sure of, he was never going to be seen as needy of someone's friendship. He extended his hand in friendship, and it was up to the other party to accept it or not accept it. Either way was going to be okay with Reg.

Having been freed up from football may have been the best thing for Reginald. His new game plan was beginning to look better all the time. From the very beginning, he had set some really lofty goals. Things had not gone as he had hoped, but with the exception of making the football team, all of the other goals remained and they were all still achievable. He had not been dealt a great hand, but like always, he was still in the game. In Reginald's mind, that was all that he had ever needed.

A Glimpse of the Budding Entrepreneur Emerges

Reginald Lewis was always a willing worker, but he looked at work and his motivation to do a job through his own personal filter. His motivation for a particular job was directly proportional to the size of the compensation. Football players on scholarships were assigned part-time jobs so they could earn pocket money and help pay a portion of their expenses. During our freshman year, Reginald and I were assigned part-time jobs working for Mr. Sam Simmons. Mr. Simmons was the athletic department custodian. He was in charge of maintenance and the upkeep of all athletic facilities, which included the old Daniel Hall Gymnasium and Rogers Stadium.

Sam Simmons had the unenviable task of making sure the athletes reported for work on time and completed their work assignments on time. This had to be verified by Mr. Simmons before they could receive their monthly paychecks. Most guys would gripe about how little money they were making, but considering how few hours most of us were putting in, it was fair compensation. Moreover, the actual work was rarely, if ever, done to Mr. Simmons's satisfaction. In this regard, Sam Simmons was one of the best men I ever knew. He was patient to a fault, and he was always understanding of your situation. Sam Simmons always looked out for the athletes. In most instances all you had to do was show up and you were paid. Whether right or wrong, Sam Simmons covered for many athletes during his time at Virginia State by making sure the work that was supposed to have been done, was actually done.

The work was not that hard, but when it came to reporting to the stadium for work, Reginald Lewis was always a "No Show." It was not that he was a slacker. Reginald Lewis could work with the best of them, but he always felt there had to be a better job and a higher payoff for his labor. He was constantly in search of the higher-paying jobs. Over the course of his time at Virginia State, he would eventually find them.

His ideal job was one that would pay him, as he loved to put it, "good money." He would always laugh whenever he used the term "good money," claiming it was a term he had picked up from his grandfather. The term had become his description of choice when referring to a wage that was above the going rate. It was the preferred level of compensation one should expect for having delivered an important service that exceeded the customer's expectations.

I never met his grandfather, but it was always evident that he was an important person in Reginald's life. In moments when it was just the two of us, he would make frequent reference to important lessons he had learned from his grandfather. This was usually at a time when he wanted to make a point about hard work and time tested work ethics.

Reginald's mother shared a story with me that revealed a small sample of the sage advice her dad had passed down to his young grandson. She said, "When Reginald began his job as a card room server in Baltimore's prestigious Suburban Club, my father pulled him aside one day and gave him this advice. He said, 'Son, when you are in the card room, help out wherever you can, but remember this. Whatever you do, stay out of the kitchen and stay out of the refrigerator. I didn't bring you out here to see you get fired over some missing hamburger.'" His grandfather's steady stream of worldly advice made an impression on Reginald.

Time spent at the Suburban Club provided him with a wealth of valuable lessons that went well beyond making "good money." It provided him with an insider's view of how Baltimore's most influential people used their playtime.

In those days, the Suburban Club catered to Baltimore's wealthiest citizens. This was young Reginald's first look at the world of the rich and powerful. The charming, attentive young black man standing in the corner of the card room was quietly acquiring a taste for the finer things in life. It is not hard to imagine Reginald Lewis lapsing into a moment of wistful thinking while carrying out his chores in the card room at the Suburban Club. I could often hear those thoughts as they began to creep into his speech. His frequent references to how the wealthy conducted themselves in their spare time was an early indication that Reginald was already starting to acquire a taste for the finer things in life.

Reg's financial situation and his quest for a job paying "good money," dictated that he become creative in finding the kind of work that best suited him. His mother, Mrs. Carolyn Fugett, recalls reminding her son that he would always have the support of his family. However, she felt it was necessary to point out that it would serve him well if he began looking for ways to increase his own stream of income. She says she told him, "Never be a person who waited for your check to come in the mail." Her message was simple: "Money will not come to you. You have to go get it." That message resonated loud and strong with Reginald. He had always worked in his spare time but he now understood that he would have to ramp things up a bit. With the extra time he gained from not having to practice and travel with the football team, Reginald worked everywhere and all the time. He began a long period, in which he worked during the school year, as a photography sales representative, bowling alley manager and encyclopedia salesman. These were jobs that paid considerably more than the stadium crew assignment. It was the kind of work that paid "good money."

Mrs. Fugett says, "This was the period when I felt Reginald Lewis the entrepreneur began to emerge." He would work like crazy during the school year and in the summer while attending summer school. Honing his money-management skills and finding new ways to earn money was now a part of the new game. The more he achieved, the greater the pride he took in his accomplishments. It was not easy, but it was a critical part of the plan. It had to be done well if he was to achieve his goal.

CHAPTER 14:

FAMILY AND FRATERNITY

"I sustain myself with the love of family."
Maya Angelou

It may have been more a reflection of the times, but both Reginald and I believed that there was a dominant posture that was appropriate for a college man. It was shoulders up, looking serious, and appearing to be in control. You had to maintain this look even when you were not in total control of events going on around you. Reginald had deep-set eyes and a thick mustache, and this standup posture created a picture of a young man who knew where he was going. He liked it that way because it left little doubt that he was always in total control of his emotions. We believed that guys who were too expressive or too openly emotional were prone to revealing personal weakness. You had to avoid appearing too excited or overly impressed by things.

This led to Reginald Lewis becoming a person who never tended toward excess when it came to passing out accolades. He was very restrained when it came to handing out praise to people. Sometimes it would seem as if he was going out of his way to appear unimpressed. This facet of his personality was universally applied. It did not matter if it was a friend, associate, or foe. If you were going to earn anything more than a casual "way to go," you were going to have to do something really special.

However, when it came to his family, he took great pleasure in making the occasional exception. He spoke of them with both pride and passion, and to me his expressions of pride in his family never quite seemed like bragging. I always knew that, for Reginald, family was special. I felt the same way about my family, so boasting about family always seemed right and proper. Even so, he was still guarded about discussing them, and he wouldn't do it with just anyone. Unless he knew you well, it was rare for him to open up about family. However, when he did speak of them, it was always with an unmistakable look of pride on his face. Whenever he mentioned any member of his family, followed by that look, I always knew what was coming next. He would usually begin with, "Hart, you are not going to believe this."

He especially loved talking about the exploits of his grandparents, uncles, siblings, and his stepfather, Jean Fugett Sr. He loved his mother too, but like most guys he was not one to talk about his mom with another guy. On this point, we were of like minds.

There was one individual who always stands out in my mind when I think of those times when Reginald was moved to speak about his family; it was his younger brother, Jean Fugett, Jr. When it came to Jean, Reginald had a special fondness for him and it was unmistakable. I have four brothers and I know brothers rarely open up about their feelings toward each other. I am not aware if Reginald ever told Jean how special he was, but I am certain he loved his little brother a lot. I am also sure he cared deeply about his other siblings too, but when we were in college it seemed as if he had a big soft spot reserved especially for Jean.

While Reg was away attending Virginia State, Jean began to break out in a big way. He was on his way to becoming a standout student/athlete at Cardinal Gibbons High School in Baltimore. I came to expect that whenever Jean accomplished something big on the athletic field or in the classroom, I was going to hear about it. Whenever there was a letter, phone call, or any form of news from home, I knew I was going to get an earful about Jean. Reginald really enjoyed sharing these accounts. Each report would begin the same way. You would see the beginnings of a smile. Reg's smile tended to reflect the level of pride he took in telling the story; the bigger the achievement, the bigger the smile. Then he would do something uncharacteristic. Reginald was not typically a close talker, but on these occasions he seemed more willing to close the distance between us. This was predictably followed by, "Hart, you won't believe what Jean did this time."

Jean was a three-sport guy with great academic and athletic skills, so Reg rarely lacked for material when giving me his report. When he first started doing this, I think he could detect a lack of enthusiasm on my part. After all, to me, Jean was just a little kid, and Reg was doing what any proud big brother would do. Over time, these reports became more frequent and each one more captivating. It seemed young Jean Fugett was making quite a name for himself on the local Baltimore sports scene, a fact that Reg would point out each time he shared a new bulletin.

As the time passed, I began to hear more about Jean from my friends back in Baltimore who were following high school sports. Soon I became less of a skeptic. I could see that Reginald's little brother was, indeed, developing into an exceptional high school athlete and an even more gifted student.

Jean would go on to finish both Cardinal Gibbons High School and Amherst College with honors. He starred as a football player at Amherst and following college he had a long successful professional football career in the NFL with the Dallas Cowboys and Washington Redskins. Today, his long list of academic, personal, and professional accomplishments is impressive. He is a successful attorney in the Baltimore-Washington area.

Enter the Brotherhood, the New Team

We had always planned that we would pledge Kappa at the beginning of the sophomore year. Pledging in those days was a tough experience. We figured the three of us pledging together would be the best way to get it done. It would put us in the best position to provide emotional and physical support for each other. Al and I had already made the commitment to pledge, beginning in the current semester. I was surprised and somewhat disappointed when Reg announced that he would wait until the second semester. I could tell Reginald was disappointed at having to watch as Al and I began our pledge work without him. I always suspected that his decision not to pledge had something to do with his grades, but as was often the case with Reg, you never knew for sure.

Between football practice and our pledge work, Al and I saw very little of Reg during September and October. For reasons that still make me shudder, life was just about to deal me a cruel hand. Half way into the pledge period, I received word from the Dean's office that there had been a mix up in my transcript from high school. My freshman grades had been good, but I fell one credit hour short of having the required number of hours to pledge. I was furious. I called upon everyone, from coaches to instructors, to plead my case, but to no avail. This was a gut punch for me. I could not stop thinking, "I'm nearly half way through the pledge period, and this happens. I've endured so much and for what?" Now I had a big decision to make. At that point, I remember thinking that, given what I knew, there was no way I was ever going to start over and go through it all again.

Fate has a funny way of working things out, because bad news for me was great news for Reginald. My being knocked off the pledge line had thrown us together again. My new roommate, Al Banks, was now fully engaged in classes, pledging, and playing football. Each of these activities were massive time consumers on their own. Taken together, they were a full-time job. Even though Al and I were roommates, there were great gaps of time when he was not around. All of a sudden, it was just like old times. Reg and I spent time hanging out together. It was almost as if we were roommates again. In fact, the way things played out that year, we actually ended up spending almost as much time together as we had spent during our freshman year.

While we were spending more time together, it soon became clear that Reginald was up to something. He began a campaign of sorts. He had concluded that I needed to pick up the gauntlet again and join him as part of the second semester's Kappa pledge line. I could certainly understand why. "Crossing those burning sands," a phrase used to describe pledging, was easier when done with a trusted friend. I had come to appreciate such a benefit when Al and I started out the year pledging together.

Still, the idea of starting all over again brought out a lot of mixed feelings for me. On the night that all my former pledge mates celebrated their coming out as freshly minted Kappa men, I did something I had never done before. Members of the fraternity, feeling a bit sorry for me, had reached out and invited me to join them in the fraternity room, where the party was in full swing. Boisterous young men and booze made for a raucous environment. At that time, I was a committed non-drinker. However, on that night I was so depressed that I took a drink. In truth, I took many drinks. For the first and only time in my life, I was flat-faced drunk.

I don't remember much of anything that happened that night, but according to Reg and Al, I had thrown a javelin at some guy in the dormitory. I was a javelin thrower on the track team, and I often kept the javelin in my room. Throwing it in the dormitory was not something I was proud of, but it provided a valuable lesson for me. Liquor does strange things to people. I decided at that moment I would never drink again. To this day, I have remained a life-long tea-totaler. Over the years, this has caused many a Kappa brother to cast a suspicious eye in my direction whenever the booze was flowing. Not taking a drink is sufficient reason to doubt the bona fides of any man claiming to be a Kappa.

When I had finally recovered from the world's longest hangover, I made my grand decision. I was going to pledge a second time. When I told Reginald my intention of going again, there was an outbreak of hand slapping, laughing, and trash talking in the room that could be heard throughout the dormitory. I had had a burning desire to become a Kappa before, but now that fire had become a raging inferno. I was more determined than ever to make it happen. Reginald and I were now ramping up our emotions to full pledge mode. This was going to be the year that we would become Kappas.

In those days, pledging for membership in an undergraduate chapter of a fraternity was a tortuous ordeal. It was an extremely intense and physically draining experience. Whether the methods were appropriate and necessary still remains a subject of much debate among those who administered them and absorbed them. Still, if you survived it, there is no denying that you learned a lot about human nature and about yourself.

By the time our pledge period was over, we had come to know ourselves in ways we had never contemplated. Strong young men who had always defined themselves by their toughness, strength, and masculinity were now being asked to become submissive. Suddenly we found ourselves having to bend to the will of other young men. This was true even though we may have deemed some of those applying the pressure to be guys who were less than our equal. That's when a thought hit like a hot towel across your face: How could they be lesser men when every one of them, including that wimpy-looking guy standing over there in the corner, had already survived this difficult ordeal?

Every man on that line had to manage his way through the simultaneous emotions of humility, anger, and fear. Such a journey would eventually provide us with valuable information, which we would apply later in life. For me, having the courage to endure, while at the same time suppressing the urge to strike back, was the ultimate test.

For Reginald Lewis, this was a powerful learning experience for a guy who had never had to subjugate himself to anyone. It wasn't about money, looks, or power. Every guy on our line wanted to become a member of this proud fraternity, but there was only one way to get it done. Membership required that every guy on that line find his own way through a tortuous myriad of emotional twists and turns. Getting through to the end meant that you had demonstrated that you had what it took to be a part of something special. When it was all over and we had made it, we all knew we had accomplished something really special. It was something only a few men could claim to have accomplished. Yes, it wasn't the Virginia State football team, but for Reginald it might as well have been. This had been a personal triumph. As a member of Kappa Alpha Psi fraternity, he was, once again, a member of an elite group of young men. It was a role that commanded real respect among students on Virginia State's campus. Best of all, this time his membership was for life. It could never be taken away by some football coach.

The night we were officially ushered into the brotherhood of Kappa Alpha Psi was a moment of immense pride for Reginald. Reginald Lewis was back where he belonged, and just watching him you could tell it felt good, very good.

I have always believed that, with the exception of graduation, that night was the happiest moment of his entire time on Virginia State's campus. Reginald was never a touchy-feely kind of guy, but that night he hugged more, laughed more, and certainly drank more than at any time before or after. That night, he proudly donned his Kappa golf cap and drank freely from the punch bowl containing a mixture of cool-aid and corn alcohol. Reginald and the rest of us partied well into the night. This was a big moment for me too, but remembering my experience with the javelin, I stayed far away from that punch bowl.

Oh, and I should mention, I came to understand the significance of those Greek letters.

CHAPTER 15:

HAVING THE NERVE TO THINK BIG

"Push yourself to set outsized goals. Falling a bit short will still leave you in a good place from which to go further."
Lin Hart

"You are who you think you are." I recall reading this quote in a book I had picked up in an airport bookstore over twenty-five years ago. It was during an excruciatingly long layover. At the time, I remember thinking, "Well, that's obvious." It didn't occur to me that this was a simple truth that many people fail to understand.

The human mind is an incredibly complex computer, and it can perform wonders. It is the conductor of the railroad we all travel on every day of our lives. It can take us to places we choose to go or, if left unattended, it can take us to places we really don't want to go. The mind does not distinguish between good, bad, or otherwise unless we take control of it. Without the right values and beliefs, the mind will usually do whatever feels good, and that can be a real problem for most of us.

Making certain you know where you want to go is the first step in getting to where you want to be. It's the destination. Your values and beliefs provide the guidance. They serve as your moral compass. The more we invest in adopting the right belief system, the more likely we are to arrive at our destination of choice. It's about using our belief system to take charge of that personal conductor that's running around inside our heads. You are who you think you are.

It was easy to see that Reginald understood how this all worked. There were many times when he was able to see a bigger opportunity, when others missed it. Where others saw biscuits and gravy, Reginald saw pheasant under glass. A good example of this occurred when Reg and I were looking for part-time work. A new bowling alley, Skylark Lanes, had just opened up in the Petersburg area. We were all excited about the prospect of getting a part-time job there. When we first walked into the place, there were a couple of other guys there, also looking for work. We all took note of the fact that that the place was under white ownership. At seeing this, our thought was the best we were going to get was a job working the counter, cleaning up, or helping out around the place.

Reg looked around the place and turned to me. He said, "Hell, I don't want to do any of that stuff. I think I can run this damn place." My thought was, "Is he serious? What had he seen that we hadn't?" A few months later, Reg was working there as the night manager. Yes, it was night manager, but at least he wasn't cleaning up the joint: He was running the place.

What Reginald Lewis always understood, was that those who achieved great success were able to do so because they were able to envision themselves achieving great success in their mind's eye. It was the crucial step in gaining firm control of the conductor.

The expression "You are who you think you are" registered with me while I was standing there, reading that book at the airport newsstand. It seemed to make a lot of sense, in trying to comprehend the full magnitude of Reginald's achievements. I've had people ask me a zillion times how Reginald Lewis was able to achieve so much. My recollection of that night at the Skylark Lanes bowling alley would always come to mind and it always led me to the same conclusion. One of the main reasons he achieved so much was because he never thought he couldn't.

The Unaffected Reginald

When I first began my speaking career, in 1994, I had the good fortune of being befriended by two of the country's top motivational speakers, Bill Coplin and Grady Jim Robinson. They had both been in the speaking business for over 20 years, but now something called the world wide web, or the internet, was just beginning to find its way into the lives of the mainstream populace. Audiences were clamoring to hear more about this new communications medium. Speakers were doing everything they could to catch up with the technology after years of having given the internet little more than passing interest. Bill and Grady both saw my background in telecommunications as a benefit, so we struck a deal. I would help them increase their understanding of the internet, and they would assist me in launching my new speaking career. In other words, we would trade on each other's mastery. It turned out to have been an ideal arrangement and it worked out well for each of us.

At that time I met Grady and Bill, they were two of the best professional speakers in the business. The key to their success had been their extraordinary acting and storytelling ability. They both had this amazing ability to craft a story and deliver it masterfully from the stage. The way they looked, the way they sounded, and the way they presented themselves allowed them to create the right impression. This, in turn, allowed them to command an entire room even when it was filled with powerful business executives. From the moment they took the stage, they became believable, memorable, and powerful. Watching these two highly respected professionals at work provided me with two very important lessons, lessons I have never forgotten:

1. You can shape both perception and reality by the way you conduct yourself. This is especially true when dealing with powerful people. Your body language, voice, and the words you choose can give you enormous control over a group.
2. Appearing unaffected when things don't go your way can provide the cover you need to survive a difficult period. To put it another way, no matter what happens on that stage, never let them see you sweat.

Here is an example of how it works when you put the two together. Let's say you are speaking to an audience of powerful business types. You deliver a joke and the audience doesn't laugh. At this point, many speakers feel the need to explain the punch line. For a speaker, that kind of behavior can lead to a slow death on stage. You have now created the impression that you're willing to beg the audience for a laugh. Powerful people don't respect begging or weakness. According to Grady and Bill, here is where you exercise your own power and control. Whenever that happens, you simply carry on with your speech and act as if you never intended for it to have been funny. Sure, it's a rough patch, but just keep right on going. Assuming you have not already delivered a stream of lousy stories, you've still got a good chance of ending your speech with a warm round of applause, rather than a resounding chorus of boos. Appearance and behavior are powerful tools when it comes to creating a successful image or the right impression.

Reginald Lewis understood that behavior and appearance worked hand in hand. When it came to creating the right impression, he applied this knowledge liberally in shaping his own image. For example, whenever he was seeking something he really wanted and didn't get it, he never threw tantrums. On the surface, it never seemed to bother him. He simply acted as though he never wanted it in the first place. This didn't mean he wasn't going to keep trying to get it, but by appearing to be unaffected, he avoided the appearance of being needy or overly reliant upon someone else's approval. He understood, as did Bill Coplin and Grady Robinson, that there was real power in being able to create the right impression.

Longtime friend Al Banks says, "One of Reginald's greatest talents was his ability to craft his image." He adds, "Reginald was always crafting his image." Al is right. The task of crafting his image was always at the forefront of Reginald Lewis's mind. He always made sure he came across as well groomed, well versed, and well in control of his emotions. No matter what you might have thought of him, it was hard to find fault with this game plan. It was part of his success-building strategy, and it was essential to him.

As good as he was at maintaining his image, there were instances when he took it to extremes. Whenever this happened, it worked against him and ended up pissing off people, even those who were his friends.

Of course, it wasn't always that way. There were moments when his gift for image building cast him in a more favorable light. Such was the case when he lost his scholarship. Prior to this having happened, I had spent countless hours sitting and listening to Reginald describe how much he wanted to be the starting quarterback on Virginia State's football team. When this dream fall apart, I knew it was not easy for him. However, I was amazed at how effective he was at appearing as though it was no big deal. As noble as it was in appearance, I knew how deep his feelings ran when it came to this subject. I had been there to witness his initial disappointment. By his own admission, throwing touchdown passes and being part of the victories had always gotten his adrenalin pumping. Now it was gone, but Reginald was not about to let anyone know the extent to which it had affected him.

Highlighting this part of his persona is not meant to be a criticism. The way he handled this episode of his life was admirable. There was never any bitching, complaining, or whining about his misfortune. At the same time as he was playing it down publicly, he was setting about recasting himself in a different light. The task confronting him required him to move forward with his life. Here, his ability to mask his emotions and appear unaffected came across as strength and an admirable quality. Once through the initial shock, he never looked back. This was Reginald's way of saying, "I get to say what's important to me, not you."

It was just as Grady and Bill had said. The great ones always have a strategy, and it's designed to create the right impression and the right image. If it doesn't turn out the way they want it to, they act as though they never expected it to turn out any other way and move on. Young Reginald may have stumbled early on in the execution of this strategy, but if you knew him, you knew he would play it until he eventually got it right.

CHAPTER 16:

THE CAMPAIGN OF 1964

"If elected, I will win."
Pat Paulsen (comedian)

If you sat down and talked with him for just a few minutes, you would soon know that Reginald Lewis saw himself as someone brimming with ideas and leadership talent. Even so, it was the spring of 1964 and he still had not shown any inclination to apply his talents while at Virginia State University. There had been plenty of opportunities in the fraternity and elsewhere on campus, but I don't recall him ever accepting or openly lobbying for any of them. While work and his studies may have been eating into his time, he seemed to have time for social events. I still thought of him as someone with lots of leadership ability. It just appeared to me that once he left the football team, he had chosen to avoid all forms of campus leadership.

As the spring semester was coming to an end, I knew there would be one last opportunity for Reginald Lewis to complete what I had always viewed as unfinished business. College fraternities and sororities are among the most fertile grounds for grooming campus leaders. The spirit of competition is something new pledges are imbued with the instant they begin their initiation rituals. Every Greek organization on campus wanted to have its fair share of campus leaders. The Kappas were no different. Among the most cherished leadership spots were the captain of the football team and the student council presidency. Following spring football practice, I was selected as co-captain of the football team. The biggest leadership plum, the election of the next year's student council president, was just around the corner. As far as I was concerned, landing both of these highly visible positions would represent a clean sweep for our fraternity. It would be even sweeter if the student council president were one of the Baltimore Guys.

Reginald had been a student council vice president in high school, so I saw this as a move that might interest him. I wasn't fooling myself, though. I knew that the idea of Reginald stepping forward was a stretch. The speculation was that he would not. Still, I wondered.

The speculation about Reginald not running proved to have been right. Reginald never tossed his hat in the ring. I may have been the only one feeling this way, but I was genuinely surprised when this happened. Reginald Lewis had taken a final pass on his opportunity to leave a leadership imprint during his four years at Virginia State.

In fairness to Reginald, he had never given me or anyone else any indication that he was interested in running for the office, and it had never been in his game plan. His plan had always been to finish Virginia State in four years and move on to law school. By now, Reginald's grades had begun to improve, and nothing was going to get in the way of him completing the plan on time.

Al Banks was ultimately selected to run for the office of Student Council President, in our senior year. As Al remembers it, he was a reluctant candidate. In a recent conversation, he told me, "I never lobbied for the nomination. I always felt like you had a hand in drafting me." I do admit to having worked at getting him nominated and elected, but I never doubted for a moment that Al was interested in running. In what was a relatively uneventful series of discussions, Al won the vote to become the fraternity's candidate for student council president in the spring of 1964. I promptly volunteered to be his campaign manager.

The Omegas, a rival fraternity, had put up two very formidable candidates for the office. Reginald, always the competitor, sensed that this election had now taken on a new flavor. It was going to be the Kappas pitted against our friendly rivals, the Omegas. Now we had ourselves a contest, and it was a contest of the highest order. To my surprise and delight, Reginald decided to join me in carrying out my campaign duties to get Al Banks elected student council president.

Once again, winning was paramount, and in his eyes the cause was great enough, even if he was not the candidate. If this was to be a contest, he was determined not to have it go on without him. He was going to get his two cents' worth into the fray. I was convinced we had the right candidate to get the job done. It was a rare moment when Reginald would get excited playing a behind the scenes role, but there he was all suited up and ready for battle.

We resorted to using one of Reginald's high school campaign maneuvers. According to Reginald, as a candidate for student council vice president at Dunbar High School, he and his running mate, Robert Bell, had plastered campaign posters throughout the hallways to focus attention on themselves. Reginald thought it would be a good idea if we did something similar during the campaign. We decided to go with the idea. At the start of the campaign, we had posters with three different photographs of Al attached to them. The three photos showed him in a suit and tie, his ROTC uniform, and his football uniform. Under each photo, I had inserted a caption. The captions read, "A scholar," "A leader," and "An athlete." It seems like a simple task today, but back then getting all those photographs produced involved some heavy lifting and toting. Without the able assistance of Herman Bell, campus photographer and fraternity brother, we would never have gotten some of this stuff done. We used photographs extensively, and Herman helped provide production, photo processing, and a quick turnaround.

As the campaign grew tighter, Reginald was right in the thick of things, offering suggestions and pitching in where he could. Election Day grew nearer, and we decided to raise the ante. Again, with the help of Herman Bell, we prepared a second set of specially designed picture posters. We decided we would put them on display the night before the election. Along with several willing fraternity brothers, we prowled the campus the night before the election putting up these picture posters everywhere. Reginald was hanging in there with us.

As the clock to Election Day was ticking down, I came up with what I thought was a brilliant idea. I proposed that we have a car caravan, right down campus Main Street, with our guy, Al Banks, as the man of the hour. This would be a last-minute surprise caravan that would have the effect of giving our guy one last shot at winning over the student body. There was just one problem. We needed a convertible car with a drop top, and who had such a car? There was instant quiet in the room, due mainly to the fact there was just two of us in the room, Reg and me. It was clear Reg did not like the direction the conversation was now taking. As far as we knew, there were only two guys on the campus with convertibles, and they were both in our fraternity. Ernie Ashford had a convertible Jaguar, and Reginald was now driving a convertible Austin-Healey. Neither car was new, but because of their make and model, both would grab the attention of the students.

My plan was to have Al prominently positioned on the back seat of Reginald's Austin-Healey as this two-car parade made its way through the streets of the main campus. It was at this point in the conversation that I began to sense I was losing Reginald. I could see in his facial expression that this idea was a definite non-starter. There was nothing more precious to Reginald than his Austin-Healey, and he wasn't about to have Al propped up on the back seat of his car.

No one made a big fuss over it, but this was the point at which Reginald's involvement in the campaign began to wane. He soon became the invisible man. He just disappeared. Upon hearing this, Al jokingly proclaimed, "Reginald did not want to donate his considerable asset, his prized Austin Healey, to something as inelegant as a campus election parade." Al was probably right. Reginald's car was his pride and joy. He wasn't going to have it used for anything other than transporting him around town. I also suspected there might have been an insurance issue. What if Al accidentally tumbled over backward and landed on his noggin? Reginald, with the foresight of a budding lawyer, would have cringed at the thought of Al suing him.

In the end, it all worked out fine. Ernie Ashford stepped in to fill the gap, and we used his Jaguar. Al's grand ride through the campus was a howling success. I'm not sure if it got us any votes, but it sure created one hell of a fuss. Whenever I think of that car caravan, I can only smile and recall the famous words of the comedian Billy Crystal, "It was simply marvelous." It was close, but Al Banks won the election.

Aside from getting Al elected student council president, there were several other unexpected, but positive outcomes from his election run. A few months prior to the start of the election period, one of my School of Business instructors, Colonel Turner, had suggested that I start interviewing with some of the recruiters who were visiting the campus. It was my junior year, and he felt this could set me up for some important follow-up interviews in my senior year. I was unaware that recruiters from AT&T and IBM had been on campus for a couple of days during most of the campaign activities. I would later find out from Colonel Turner that several recruiters had inquired about the campaign and the students who had direct involvement in it.

I had a previously scheduled meeting with recruiters from AT&T following our car caravan. During the interview, the recruiters focused most of their attention on football and the fact that I had been selected captain of the football team. In an effort to refocus them, Colonel Turner stuck his head in the doorway and said, "That guy you're talking to is the campaign manager for the guy you saw riding in that Jaguar."

Colonel Turner had intervened on my behalf and in doing so had set in motion a series of life-changing events for me. The recruiters were now curious about my role as the campaign manager and my views on leadership outside of football. Colonel Turner's timely intervention had triggered an entirely new conversation. It also opened up a window of opportunity for future interviews. AT&T's recruiters would later arrange for a follow-up interview the next year, which was to be my senior year. Those second interviews ultimately led to me being hired by AT&T following my graduation. It was the beginning of a wonderful career with Western Electric and AT&T that lasted nearly 30 years. I retired in 1995 as AT&T Network Systems' Director of International Engineering. Working for AT&T Network Systems gave me the opportunity to serve in a wide range of executive roles with responsibilities in the United States and abroad.

There was another irony in the events surrounding the "Great Campaign of 1964." Al Banks was called to the placement office later that same day. He interviewed with the Department of Labor, and the interview resulted in him receiving a summer internship. Al said, "That summer internship was one of the best work experiences I ever had."

I can't confirm that there was a connection to the campaign, but Reginald Lewis would later receive a job offer from IBM, which he turned down.

The Love Doctor

Throughout these early years, Reginald had come to fancy himself as a real ladies' man. The problem was that of his claims of numerous conquests, none could ever be confirmed because he always operated in such a clandestine manner. No one ever knew where he was or what he was doing. That never stopped him from making the claims, but frequently it would open the window to reveal his well-guarded sense of humor. I used the term "well-guarded" because there were times when Reginald worked so hard at crafting his image that he ended up suppressing the parts of his personality that made him a likable guy. Often missing in action was his sense of humor.

An example of this occurred shortly after the start of our senior year. It was October 1964, and I was just at the start of a serious courtship with Frances Washington. Frances was an attractive senior from Winchester, Virginia. My roommate, Al Banks, was dating Karel Cobb, who was Frances's roommate. As luck would have it, they invited Frances and me to join them on a double date.

Before long, Frances and I were seeing each other on a regular basis. It wasn't long before Reginald got wind of it. One afternoon he stopped me on campus and began offering me advice on how to sustain my new relationship. What made it especially odd was that this advice was coming from a guy who, for as long as I had known him, espoused the virtues of avoiding a serious relationship. Now here he was, acting like "The Love Doctor."

He began giving me a speech about how he thought Frances was the perfect match for me. He said, as my friend, it was his duty to make certain I did not mess things up. He went on to add that his considerable experience with women made him the ideal advisor in this situation, and best of all, his services would be offered free of charge. When he said his services would be free, I knew he was putting me on. Reginald Lewis never did anything for free. He could not resist the urge to break out laughing, all of which made it obvious he was not serious. Reginald had the most infectious laugh, and it could go on forever if the joke was especially funny. I often wondered how many people ever got to see that side of Reginald Lewis. I suspect not nearly as many as there should have been.

Reginald always thought of Frances as the right choice for me. The following year, when we announced we were getting married, he playfully reminded me that I should be forever indebted to him for helping me navigate the precarious route to matrimony. I did think it was special of him to take such an interest in our courtship. I think he actually believed his unsolicited intervention was a critical part of the process in moving us along. Who knows? Maybe it was. But what Reginald didn't know was that I had held a secret crush on Frances since our freshman year. It had taken me three years to get up the courage to act on it. Convincing me that Frances Washington was the right woman for me may have been the easiest sale Reginald F. Lewis ever made.

CHAPTER 17:

THE FINAL DASH TO THE FINISH LINE

"If you don't design your own life plan, chances are you'll fall into someone else's plan. And guess what they have planned for you...Not Much!"

Jim Rohn

Maybe it was because we were all getting older, but the summer between our junior and senior years seemed to come and go in a flash. Reginald was still sticking to his regular routine of attending summer classes at Virginia State. Whenever he was not in class, he was some place working. Since the end of his freshman year, this had been his regular routine. It made it possible for him to boost his grades and keep him on track for graduation in four years while also accumulating a few bucks for the coming semester. This routine had a worked well for him.

When the school year began, it felt like everyone was in a headlong dash toward graduation in the spring. For the better part of the past two years, Reginald had lived off campus. Now he was back on campus, living in Puryear Hall. I would only see him infrequently, usually during his occasional visits to the fraternity table in the dining hall. He was still not a big fan of the campus dining hall but would occasionally sit and chat before heading off to class.

All signs pointed to him having made substantial improvements in his grades during his junior year. In the past, he had rigidly adhered to his practice of remaining close-mouthed whenever the subject of grades would come up. Now he seemed more relaxed and willing to pull back his veil of secrecy. He spoke more openly about his grades. Things were starting to look up for Reg.

Thanksgiving and Christmas would pass quickly. Along with them went the cold days and nights of winter. We were now into the budding flowers and the warm glow of spring 1965. This is when Virginia State campus was at its best. Our time there, as students, was rapidly coming to an end.

Reg still wasn't sure how he was going to achieve the most critical step in the final leg of his plan. This was the part that involved selling himself as a candidate for law school. He was now spending a lot of time in Virginia Hall, the administration building, checking his grades and making certain all of his records were in order. At the same time, he was working the relationship angle full time. Anyone willing to write and say positive things about him became a prospect. Reginald knew, even with the progress of his junior year, that his transcript would likely become an obstacle in his gaining admittance to one of the elite law schools. In his search to find ways to bolster his prospects, he sought the support of every well-positioned faculty member, school official, or friend who might speak well of him. One of the friends he sought out for help was Herman Bell, a fraternity brother.

Herman recalls how Reginald had approached him to solicit his father's help in applying for admission to the University of Pennsylvania's law school. Herman's dad had graduated from there in the late 1940s, following the war. At the time of Reginald's request, Herman's father was a practicing attorney and a person of considerable influence. At one point in his career, he served as the deputy attorney general for the state of New Jersey. According to Herman, his father was unsuccessful in his bid to help Reginald.

As everyone was scrambling toward graduation in the spring, I realized I would have to spend an extra semester on campus. The time was nearing when I would have to make up for having changed my major, following my first year rooming with Reginald Lewis. It turned out to have been a great

move, but now I would find myself nine hours short of graduation. Still, there was one bit of good fortune that would prove
to be enough to keep me pumped up. I had been drafted
by the professional football team the Buffalo Bills following
the close of my senior year. I was really excited about the
prospect of putting in a full summer of training and having
a chance to make the team. More important, thanks to the
bonus money that came with signing my contract, I finally
had more than two quarters to rub together. As my dad used
to say, "It feels a whole lot better when you can get your hands
on some folding money." My old man knew what he was talking about. For someone who had been perpetually broke
throughout college, this was a rare but welcome experience.

As we were nearing the final lap, Reginald began talking
about a new summer program he had heard about at Harvard. It was being funded by the Rockefeller Foundation.
The program's goal was to introduce non-graduating minority students to a law school environment. As a secondary goal,
it would serve as a means of gaining exposure to Harvard and
its law school. Officials at Harvard had become aware of the
small number of minority students applying for law school admission. The hope was that this summer program would provide them with valuable experience as well as whetting their
appetite for law as a career path. Reginald said he was trying
to gain acceptance into the program. I didn't find out until
years later that technically, as a graduating senior, Reginald
was not eligible for this program. Nonetheless, he proceeded
to press every lever possible to gain the necessary support to
have his name submitted by officials at Virginia State. He was

determined to make Harvard Law School his next stop after graduating from Virginia State.

Upon hearing all this, I knew there were two things you could count on. First, by hook or by crook, he was going to get into that program. The second thing was that, other than family and a few close friends, no one would know before the last minute how the process was going.

Ultimately, his dogged determination ended in success. He convinced his professors and the officials at Virginia State that his name should be included among those submitted to Harvard. He would be rewarded for his efforts. When the selection process was finally over, Harvard selected Reginald as a member of their summer program. A short time afterwards, I heard from him. He was excited as heck to share his good news. This was a special moment for him. Our conversation was reminiscent of the one we had four years earlier, when he called to announce that he had received a scholarship to attend Virginia State and we were going to be teammates. The enthusiasm, passion, and pride that he had expressed when playing football had once again returned to his voice. However, this time we were not going to be teammates. This time he would be going solo.

Over the past four years, things had not always gone well for Reginald, but here he was still standing, still talking trash. He had climbed all the way back from one of the biggest disappointments in his life. He had failed to make Virginia State's football team and live out his dream of becoming the conquering hero he had been in high school. He had worked his butt off, trying to cushion the blow of losing the financial support that came with his scholarship. I had been there to witness it all. Not many people were in a position to fully appreciate the steep climb he had to make in order to get to this point in his life. He certainly never displayed it publicly. Reginald was now nearing the final phase of his climb, and you could hear the joy and elation in his voice.

Still, not all was done. I would later find out that there were no guarantees attached to Harvard's summer program. Reginald said it was not intended to be an automatic doorway to Harvard Law School. It didn't seem to matter. Since that summer in 1956, when I first met him, I had watched this guy grow in stature and in confidence. As he spoke, I could hear it in his voice. Not having a doorway was not going to be a deterrent to him gaining admission into Harvard Law School. I knew, in the summer of 1965, the folks at Harvard were about to be bowled over by this runaway train, in the person of Reginald F. Lewis. I had seen him work this route before. Once inside the gates of Harvard University, he was going to deploy his charm, his guile, and his incredible ability to present the details of his case. In doing so, he was going to blast open his own pathway. What may have appeared to some as obstacles were about to become doorways that would soon swing wide open and welcome one of Virginia State's graduates to Harvard Law School. In the fall of 1965, Reginald F. Lewis was admitted.

His tendency to keep grinding away until he found a way to succeed had worked again. In his unfinished autobiography, Reginald relates the story of how he was actually attending classes as a freshman Harvard Law School student before school officials realized he had not officially filled out an application for admission. By his own account, this was a first time such an oversight had ever occurred in Harvard's long and storied history. Harvard, meet Mr. Reginald F. Lewis.

In the years, that followed Reginald's graduation from Harvard Law School in 1968, we saw each other infrequently. We stayed in contact by phone and mail. In 1973, I was working for Western Electric. The company had agreed to an arrangement that allowed me to spend 18 months working as a national program director with the National Alliance of Business. My office was located in Washington, D.C., on K Street, in the heart of the lobbyists' district. Reginald began showing up there periodically, and whenever he did, he would drop by. For a while, my office was quite the place to be. I reported to the late General John Condon. John was a highly decorated hero for valor in World War II. He played an important role in helping plan General Douglas MacArthur's Pacific campaign. General Condon reported to the former General Motors executive John DeLorean, later the storied creator of the iconic DeLorean automobile. He had joined the National Alliance of Businessmen as its top executive shortly after I arrived in Washington. The Watergate complex, located just a few blocks away, was just about to erupt into an historic scandal that would eventually lead to the impeachment of President Nixon. It was an exciting time to be in Washington, D.C. Reginald recognized that the world was changing fast and that many of the roads to progress were leading to Washington, and from there to the rest of the world. He had begun to look toward the capital as a key place to make both business and legal connections.

The Art of the Surprise

As his career progressed, there would be moments when I would encounter a look of puzzlement on the faces of people who were amazed by the sheer breadth of Reginald's business achievements. Accompanying that look was always the question, "Who is Reginald F. Lewis and where did he come from?" To my surprise, some of those in amazement were people who had been students on Virginia State's campus when Reginald was there, but had little or no recollection of him as a student. Regardless of who they were or where they had been, they were all surprised by the magnitude of his accomplishments.

A close inspection of his life will reveal that Reg loved using, the art of surprise. It was one of the main reasons so many Wall Street pundits were caught cold, like stunned prizefighters, on August 6, 1987, when his purchase of the $2 billion Beatrice empire was announced. The question they were all asking was, "Who is this guy and where has he come from?" Reginald had remained under the radar on purpose, choosing to wait until the closing moments of the deal before revealing himself as the buyer. It was a move done to conceal his intentions and achieve the maximum shock value. In that case, it made good business sense to wait in the wings. However, I suspect the delayed shock effect of doing what no one thought he was capable of doing was an incredible high for

Reg. Waiting until the last minute also had the added benefit of allowing him to, as they say on Wall Street, "surprise to the upside." No one liked surprising to the upside more than Reginald Lewis did.

Following his emergence as the central figure behind the Beatrice deal, he was quoted in the *New York Times* of March 20, 1988, as saying, "I'm not much for making a big splash about things. I really do prefer to operate quietly."

Translation: "I like shocking the hell out of people."

The Wall Street pundits weren't the only ones he left swinging in the wind. In the summer of 1987, a couple of months before the Beatrice deal was announced, I was in New York on business. As I had on so many other visits to New York, I called his office. He was out of town, but later he returned my call. The conversation began like most of our calls. There were the usual questions. How is business? How is the family? What brings you to New York? After getting past all the perfunctory stuff, he said, "Hart, I'm working on something. Man, you're not going to believe it. It's really big, but I can't tell you about it." My next comment was one I had uttered many times before: "If you can't tell me, why the heck did you bring it up?" He let out a big laugh, saying, "You'll read all about it in the *Wall Street Journal* when it's finally done." I remember thinking to myself, "Reg's doing it again." He was ratcheting up the tension before breaking out the big moment of surprise.

By now, I had come to understand that when he said something like this, he was not just blowing smoke. Something big was about to happen, and I knew it would be pointless to probe for more details. Moreover, there was something inside me that would not allow me to grovel or beg for more information. The mere fact that he was telling me this much I saw as an indication of our years of friendship. He was right about one thing. When I did find out about it, I was reading the *Wall Street Journal*. No one enjoyed surprising an unsuspecting public more than Reginald F. Lewis.

An Ordinary Guy with Extraordinary Goals

In many ways, Reginald F. Lewis was an ordinary guy. His distinction was that he spent his lifetime pursuing extraordinary goals.

Was he the smartest person I ever met? For sure, he was not and he knew it. On rare occasions, he would even admit it. He understood that success is determined by many factors. Among the most important were clear vision, determination, hard work, and timing. To use a gambling metaphor, "when the chips were on the table," Reginald was going to use these attributes to maximize his chances of winning. Whether it was information, money, relationships, or skills, whatever he needed he went after it, and he got it. In all the years that I knew him, the one word that describes him best is "determined." His desire to excel extended far beyond the expectations of most people and serves as the main reason why he achieved so much in his lifetime.

Leon Stewart, a former teammate of Lewis's at Dunbar High School, says the thing that stood out in his memory was how well Reginald was able to play three sports, keep up with his classes, and work at part-time jobs.. He says, "Reginald Lewis was not a guy who hung out a lot, and he was a hard, hard worker." Stewart recalls that in his time at Dunbar, he could only recall two people in the entire school with a car and a driver's license. He was one, and Reginald was the other. Stewart's point was that Reginald wanted the special benefits that came with getting his education and having a car, and he was willing to pay the price for having both..

Stewart says he always knew Reginald would be successful. On this point, we both agree. From the very first time I met Reginald, I could tell he was going to be successful, but my expectations were well short of what he actually achieved. I have discussed this with others who knew him, and I was not alone in underestimating him. He exceeded far beyond everyone's expectations, except those of his own.

Reginald always carried around in his head this vision of himself as a big time leader with the calculating instincts of a riverboat gambler. One of the biggest riverboat gamblers of our youth was the stoop shouldered, bow legged quarterback of the Baltimore Colts, named Johnny Unitas.

Reginald was fond of rambling on about how our hometown heroes, the Baltimore Colts, had beaten the New York Giants in the 1956 NFL Championship game. This was one of Reg's proudest sports moments. He would always add a couple of tag lines to suggest he understood the game in a way that most did not. He would point out the significance of the Colts having won the game in the Big Apple, "New York," rather than in Baltimore. While he may have used different words at the time, Reginald would go to great lengths to explain that winning the championship in New York was a "force multiplier." His thesis was that New York was the biggest stage in the world, thus making the win a much bigger deal. He was on to something back then. Many now consider that game to have been the "Greatest Football Game Ever Played," mainly because it was one of the first NFL games played on the national TV stage and beamed across the country from New York.

New York always held a special attraction for Reginald. In his view, it was the place to be. He also knew that winning a big game on a big stage, like New York, required doing more than just learning the rules of the game and playing hard. The pressure of competing in a place with the demands of New York required that you be able to survive long enough to learn how to play the game.

The featured star of that 1956 National Football League championship game, Baltimore's quarterback Johnny Unitas, was one of the greatest survivalist of that time. He was, without question, one of the most unlikely stars in the history of modern sports. As such, he became something of a model for Reginald. Unitas was tough, capable, and demanded nothing short of excellence from those on his team. He understood the rules of playing on a big stage , and because he did, his team had survived the hot lights, unrelenting pressure, and the harsh scrutiny of New York City.

Reginald had always visualized himself playing quarterback in a big game on a much bigger, grander field than most would have imagined when we were growing up. New York suited him well. In his own way, Reginald F. Lewis was determined to replicate the success of his hometown hero Johnny Unitas. He was going to plant his stake in New York City, set the bar high, and proceed to go well above it. One can only imagine how high he might have gone had he not been stricken in the prime of his life.

The Good Must Never Become the Enemy of the Great

Many years later, I recall picking up what I believe to have been one of the best books ever written on business leadership. It was authored by Jim Collins. The book's title was *Good to Great.* It became a best-seller. It still ranks high on the list today. In his book, Collins proposed a very simple but thought-provoking idea. He advanced the notion that the best business leaders consistently inspired their companies to high levels of performance because they resisted the temptation to settle for being good enough. According to Collins, yielding to that temptation resulted in the kind of thinking that ultimately assigns companies to the trash bin of mediocrity. It's the same with people. By not pushing the limits of our competency, we allow the good to become the enemy of great. Some refer to this as the "Curse of Competence."

After I finished reading the book, I set it aside, thinking "Good to Great?" That's the best description I ever came across to describe young Reginald Lewis. Much of what he did back then was carefully crafted to take him beyond good, to achieve something great. It may have been difficult for some to see, back them, but later in his life the force of his commitment to greatness would become more evident. From the very beginning, Reginald's goal was never about becoming good. It had always been about becoming great.

On his road to greatness there were those who came to know both his highly combustible side and his more personable side. I learned, very early, that the best way to deal with Reginald was to meet him wherever I found him. What I mean is that there were times when it came down to who could argue the loudest and the longest. Ultimately, we always found terms upon which we could co-exist as friends.

In fairness to Reginald, history has long recorded that hard-charging, successful entrepreneurs frequently made life difficult for those close to them. The names Steven Jobs and Bill Gates come to mind, just to name two. When they were in the process of building their global enterprises, there were few who would have described either of them as being easy to deal with. However, in the final analysis, history tends to judge such high achievers in light of the circumstances that confronted them during their climb to greatness. The backward look of history also provides additional insight into the unique attributes that contributed to their greatness.

Reginald's oversized ambition was matched by a set of personal attributes that fit neatly with his drive for success:

- The courage of his convictions. When he felt he was right, there was no moving him. It often bordered on stubbornness, but often he was right.

- The ability to think big. He was always willing to expand the range of what was possible. A downside of this may have been his tendency to render harsh judgment on those who did not share his outsized imagination of what was possible.

- Rigorous self-discipline. His disciplined approach in matters of importance, both large and small, resulted in him being extremely good at sticking with his plan. His belief system revolved around planning his work and working to his plan.

- Personal charm. He understood and made effective use of his personal charm. Armed with his trademark gap-tooth smile and a healthy dose of chutzpah, he could turn on the charm at any moment. When it came to interesting conversation, he was a worthy discussion partner for anyone, especially those professing to have been brilliant or academically gifted.

- Ability to focus. His ability to focus allowed him to look well below the surface and sort through the minutiae of detail required to reveal the real opportunity. Knowing how the pieces came together was his chosen method for finding the keys to the castle.

CHAPTER 18:

THE FINAL CHAPTER AND THE
LAST NOTE

"The laws that govern our circumstances are abolished by new circumstances."
Napoleon Bonaparte

On January 18, 1992, Reginald wrote the following note to me. I have always found it to have been ironic that he chose to write it exactly one year and one day before the date of his death. He passed away on January 19, 1993.

In the note he spoke of our past debates, of which there were many, and offered his view of the emerging global economy. It was evident that he was beginning to see that the world was approaching a critical inflection point. We were about to witness the launching of a period of unprecedented change, and it was going to occur at an exponential rate. He understood that grasping the implications of such change could provide serious "first mover" advantages for those businesses on the leading edge of change. This note clearly indicates that just before his death he was making plans to leverage the benefits of his global experience and the global presence of his enterprise.

REGINALD F. LEWIS

1/18/92

Dear Lin,

Great to hear from you. Trust things are going well for you and the entire family. Yes, I am pleased with my progress, especially now that I am operating internationally. Europe is quite a place to be just now. Economic integration is a reality in many respects already and political integration will probably occur in our lifetimes. I remember well some of our debates in college and our interchanges certainly toughened me then for the hard battles ahead. All the best.

Reg

Reginald F. Lewis

1/18/92

Dear Lin,

Great to hear from you. Trust things are going well for you and the entire family. Yes, I am pleased with my progress, especially now that I am operating internationally. Europe is quite a place to be just now. Economic integration is a reality in many respects already and political integration will probably occur in our lifetime. I remember well some of our debates in college and our interchanges certainly taught me then for the hard battles ahead — all the best,

9 West 57th Street, 48th Floor, New York, New York 10019

This was the last written communication I would ever receive from Reginald. It was hand written exactly one year and a day before his untimely death in 1993.

From reading his note, it was clear that Reginald Lewis was beginning to understand that the world was in the initial stages of dramatic change. Those who intended to be players on a global stage would have to act fast if they wanted to stay ahead of the changes. He knew that information and the speed of communication would soon become the new currencies of the 21st century. Reg was already making plans to become a significant "first mover" in a world that was moving toward his strength, the appetite for digging through every scrap of information for understanding.

Throughout his life, Reginald always viewed himself as a difference maker. He believed any team would be better with him on it. He wanted to leave his mark on the world. In the end, he did. At the time of his death, Lewis was the wealthiest black man in history and one of the most successful entrepreneurs of all time. He was the CEO of a commercial empire that spanned four continents. His personal fortune was estimated to have been in excess of $400 million.

Throughout this book, I have made many references to Reginald's preference for working in the background, rather than seeking public attention. Reginald had been ill for some time, yet he had managed to keep it out of the print media and off the airwaves until the very last minute. When the news of his death became public, it was a shock to everyone, which was more than a little ironic. No one enjoyed surprising people with big and shocking news more than Reginald F. Lewis did. His exit from the stage for the final time had provided him with one last time to shock and stun the world and no one enjoyed shocking the world with big news more than Reginald F. Lewis did.

In Conclusion

A good deal has already been written about Reginald F. Lewis, yet little has been written, in detail, about the years highlighted in this book. This became clear to me when I traveled the country as a professional speaker and the same question would come up repeatedly: "What was Reginald like before he became rich?" Questions like this tended to confirm my long-held belief that these were critical years, and as someone who lived through them I needed to write about them. In life, Reginald F. Lewis was many things to many people. This was my opportunity to share my story and provide another perspective from which to view Reginald F. Lewis's incredible accomplishments. It recounts a period that very few people, outside of his family, were a part of. Having been one of the privileged few, I felt compelled to write about as it happened.

It was during these years that Reginald F. Lewis first began probing and testing the ideas that would eventually make him a person of considerable accomplishment and wealth. It was during these years that he determined that he had a mountain to climb if he wanted to go from being ordinary to extraordinary.

There are many messages embedded between the pages of this book. However, there is one that I know Reginald would have wanted me to impart to my younger readers. Young Reginald Lewis never stopped dreaming. He never flinched from doing the hard work required to achieve his extraordinary goals and dreams. In many ways, this is the theme of this entire book. The driving force for that theme is something Reginald was known to make frequent reference to. It was advice he would freely offer whenever he was asked to give an account of how he had managed to achieve so much over the course of his life. Reginald's response was that simple yet powerful bit of advice, "Keep going, no matter what."

My hope is that, by reading this book, you will also be inspired to "Keep going, no matter what." If that happens, then the best purposes of my having written this book will have been served.

THE DAY AFTER HIS DEATH, THE FOLLOWING ARTICLE APPEARED IN THE NEW YORK TIMES:

Reginald F. Lewis, 50, Is Dead; Financier Led Beatrice Takeover

Published: January 20, 1993

"Reginald F. Lewis, a Wall Street lawyer and financier who was one of the nation's richest businessmen and a prominent corporate takeover dealer, died yesterday in Manhattan, one day after his company announced he was suffering from brain cancer. He was 50 and lived in Manhattan and Paris.

Mr. Lewis died from a cerebral hemorrhage related to the cancer, his company said.

Mr. Lewis, whose $1 billion acquisition in 1987 of the Beatrice Companies, a foods concern, led to the formation of his own company,

TLC Beatrice International, had amassed personal assets of $400 million, according to estimates by Fortune magazine. By acquiring the Beatrice operations, TLC, which stands for The Lewis Company, became the largest company in the country run by a black person."

The story of Reginald F. Lewis's remarkable life beyond the years covered in this book can be read in his autobiography, *Why Should White Guys Have All the Fun?* It was co-written with the author Blair S. Walker and with Reginald providing his personal contributions shortly before his death.

HIGHLIGHTS OF REGINALD F. LEWIS'S LEGACY

- The Reginald F. Lewis School of Business, Virginia State University
- The Reginald F. Lewis Museum of Maryland African-American History & Culture
- The Reginald F. Lewis Kappa Alpha Psi Inc., Alpha Phi Chapter Alumni Endowed Scholarship Fund
- The Reginald F. Lewis International Law Center at Harvard Law School
- Reginald F. Lewis High School of Business & Law, Baltimore, Maryland
- The Lewis College in Sorsogon City, Philippines
- Why Should White Guys Have All The Fun? by Reginald F. Lewis & Blair S. Walker

CPSIA information can be obtained at www.ICGtesting.com
Printed in the USA
LVOW07s0225100414

381130LV00010B/99/P